Think Ideas

And

Create Wealth

I0481153

The Secret in Developing
Ideas Worth Millions

Patricia Orlunwo Ikiriko

First published in 2017 by Patricia Orlunwo Ikiriko

pikiriko@hotmail.com

www.patriciaikiriko.com

Cover design by Peter Okomota

Legal Disclaimer

In regards to the topics and issue covered, the author has done her best to ensure that all information contained in this publication is accurate and is up to date as far as possible as at the date of publication. She does not warrant or represent at any time that the contents within are accurate due to the rapid development and change variation.

While every attempt has been made to verify the information provided in this book, the author takes no responsibility for errors, omissions or inaccuracies. The author is not liable for any actions that may result from the information contained within this publication.

The author shall not be held liable to any party or person for any, indirect, special, incidental, direct or any other consequential damages arising from use of the information contained in this publication. The material is provided "as is" and without warranties.

Book Review

I must recommend you to read this book to develop your ideas. Patricia does a thorough work in explaining the basic principles how to get into the right mindset for wealth creation on "Trajectory Model for Personal Success". It is engaging and a MUST read for young entrepreneurs. If the content of the model is followed with dedication, it will surely translate to success.

Paul James

Entrepreneur leadership Inc.

United State

Your words are a new "golden rule" for young people. If they take the time to read this work, they will learn who they are, and have fuel to inspire themselves to greatness.

Bill

Eagle2442 Co. Limited

United State

Absolutely a must read resource for young people who want to build their own business. Lots of great ideas for you to transform your potential to wealth; Patricia talks about something that is so important to driving success in idea creation, it provides refreshing ideas and thoughts on strategies to generate ideas to create product. The book is great to understanding the basics of strategy to developing your own ideas to establish your business.

Mr Alebiosu Adebola (B.ENG.,PGDE)

Abuja

F.CT, Nigeria

Dedication

My husband, Hon (Evang) Hope Odhuluma Ikiriko, for his love and continuous support; to my loving children, Doxa Chiudushime and Chanan-Christie Ikiriko for their unending support; to my beloved grandniece Analyn Chibib, and my niece Oforo Danny Johnson.

Acknowledgements

I thank my loving father God Almighty for giving me the inspiration to empower young people in this generation to create wealth.

My best friend and husband Hon Hope Odhuluma Ikiriko

Preface

Every young person is talented with great potential to shine, not to suffer frustration, humiliation or lack. As a matter of fact, every young people in the present generation can be said to be celebrity, someone the world should celebrate because of the wealth of technological exposure to information to generate great idea at fingertip to make wealth.

The essence of this book originated out of my desire to empower young people, is about affecting your world positively and making the most of your life. It is an experiential blue print for **creating unique ideas**, a process you can immerse yourself in having deep insight into your potential, so to speak - that you can think about– that you can be experimenting – studying – reflecting-- to create your own idea.

This book is a powerful informative nugget to **ensure that you create wealth with**

simple ideas to live an outstanding life. Information is a great asset in the world of success and power that can keep you ahead! **You must be informed to be transformed**, because you cannot get any idea higher than you are informed.

Over the course of more than 15 years, including challenging personal ordeals and sometimes difficult conversations, I developed Patricia Ikiriko's Trajectory Model for Personal Success, a solid foundation for generating ideas to develop multiple streams of income. I have worked with hundreds of people who generously shared their stories about working with young people. Many affirmed that the challenge with young people isn't inadequate genetic asset, but their inability to tap into what is already within. Some clarified that every individual has potential for greatness and the ability to tap into what is within to create idea, but the interplay is how they can be influence to excel with powerful blend of instruction, encouragement, and constant practice to create products or services to generate multiple streams of income.

The skills needed for successful achievement are ultimately gained only through knowledge acquisition at every level. Alexander Graham Bell explained that it is the man who carefully advances step by step with his mind becoming wider and wider, who is bound to succeed in the greatest degree. Skills don't hatch fully formed from birth, but are nurtured. They evolve and mature through practice, trial and error, feedback from others, information, and personal reflections as you move through the different stages of life. Thomas Edison attested that success is the product of several kind of mental and physical application.

How to use the book

Taking into consideration the mindset of young people and the effort of teachers, trainers and coaches, the contents of this book are divided into three parts for deeper insights that underlie all changes that create reality about generating a great idea that could potentially be worth millions:

- **Part 1: How to generate ideas**

This first part is a success manual to make your life extraordinary, that exposes simple processes great inventors and innovators that changed business and personal life in the world used, which you too can apply in idea creation. This section discloses how to make your ideas authentic, a compass to help you navigate through the pathway to generate ideas for products or services.

- **Part 2: Maximising your success**

The second part reveals top secrets to leverage opportunities that help you to become optimistic rather than pessimistic of your potential, with no barrier mind-set. The methods explores the major factors that motivate all positive changes, decisions, and choice for taking control of your life to unleashing your incredible potential that make up for personal success to developing multimillion ideas.

- **Part 3: Action strategies**

The third part reveals how to live with vision of your idea in mind, and practical step by step model of using your ideas to creating products and services to develop your financial freedom.

This exposes *exactly what you are looking for to solve your problem*, to bringing innovation to existing concepts, thinking of it as comparable to telling a story connecting a problem and a solution in that niche.

Table of Contents

Preface   **8**

Introduction   **21**

Section 1: How to generate ideas   **31**

Chapter 1: Ten Simple Steps To Create Ideas For Invention   **32**

Imagination leads to success   40

Turning your challenges into great ideas   43

Essential points in creating your ideas   53

Your idea generation decision today   55

Chapter 2: Dreaming the seeds of your success   **57**

Aspiration and Purpose   62

The decision concerning your dream today   71

Chapter 3: Why ideas are so important   **73**

What decision have you made on the importance of your idea today?   81

Chapter 4: Listening to your inner voice to create ideas   83

7 steps to creating ideas from your inner voice

    86

1. Exchange negative thoughts: 86

2. Redefinition: 87

3. Meditate: 88

4. Be passionate: 89

5. Focus: 90

6. Be true to yourself: 91

7. Pay attention: 91

Chapter 5: The dynamics of desire for achieving end-results   96

A burning desire for awakening great ideas   97

Success: 101

Pride: 102

Recognition: 103

Assessing oneself: 103

Financial Freedom: 104

Your decision on your desire today   106

Chapter 6: Developing ideas from inspiration 109

Capture your idea 116

Your inspiration decision today 118

Chapter 7: Generating ideas for creating products and services 120

Study your market: 121

Existing products: 121

Fellow individuals: 122

Knowledge: 123

Objects: 124

Routine: 125

Your idea generation decision today 126

Chapter 8: Enabling creativity and innovation from simple thoughts 129

Believe in yourself: 132

Mental Exercising: 133

Think from a different perspective: 134

Imagination: 135

Moment of Reflection: 136

Benefit of thoughts   137

Model for developing simple thoughts   140

Your idea generation decision today   142

Chapter 9: Making your vision a reality144

Put it on paper: 148

Draft the strategy: 149

Break down the plan: 149

Evaluate the process: 150

Your decision on vision today   157

Chapter 10: Developing resilience and strategy to overcome limitation   160

Your decision to develop resilience and strategy to overcome limitation today   169

Chapter 11: Sourcing and developing the content   172

Ways of sourcing content for your idea   175

Mindmapping   181

Ways of preparing your content ideas to be accepted   183

Making your idea authentic   185

Model experts' ideas in your niche   188

Your decision to sourcing and developing
content today   189

Section 2: Maximising your success   191

**Chapter 12: How do you make most of your
potential?   192**

What is a trajectory?   196

My Trajectory Model   199

1. WHO?   200

2. WHY?   207

3. WHAT?   213

4. WHERE?   218

5. WHOM?   222

6. WHEN?   226

7. VISION   229

Your decision to make most of your potential
today   249

Chapter 13: Ideas from young minds that have changed the world   251

Young people who have realised their great ideas.   254

Your decision on ideas from young minds that changed the world today   278

Section 3: Action Strategies   281

Chapter 14: Action   282

The dog blanket   282

How To Effectively Maintain Your Action Plan   285

Managing stress   286

Chapter 15: How to turn your life around   289

Turnaround steps: 290

Self-diagnosis   290

Identifying barriers   292

Action exercise   293

Dreams   297

Action exercise   299

Consider your daily priorities   299

Setting your outcome   300

How To Maximise The Best Within   302

Your Decision To Turn Your Life Around Today
                                              316

Chapter 16: Goal-setting   **318**

Definition   318

Action exercise: Goal-Setting activity   320

Model for Achieving Your Idea   322

Utilising The Power Of The Morning   330

How to Make Vision Board for Your Idea on
computer   336

8 Tips to Achieve Your Ideas Faster   337

Your decision on goal-setting today   339

Conclusion: Last words   **341**

Unlock your potential   341

Transformation Action   348

References   349

About the Author   357

Introduction

"No matter what people tell you, words and ideas can change the world" – *Robin Williams.*

What is an idea?

An idea could be explained as a simple thought or collection of thoughts that generate in the mind, a suggestion as to a possible course of action. It could be produced with intent, but sometimes it can also be generated unintentionally.

Ideas are part of our everyday vocabulary. Virtually everything we use in our daily lives came from an idea. My main aim in writing this book is to show you the methodology involved in developing an idea that could be worth millions. This process is rarely taught in school, or by parents and guardians, yet they help young people in discovering their potentials for achieving financial freedom. The big emphasis is on how to discover your uniqueness, capacity, innate-ability, and what you have within you to generate great **ideas**. It is also about how to overcome your fears in order to develop a **vision** of what you want to achieve in life. This book will show you how to unlock your passion, abundance and purpose in life.

Vision is vital if you want to succeed. The height you can see is the height you will attain; you cannot go beyond your vision. Personally, I understand vision as a picture of what I can achieve ("what can be") rather than what I am seeing presently ("what is"). I created 'Young and Influential' as my life-vision to help young people worldwide to develop their potential by using their ideas to create their own business... like Mark Zuckerberg, who created a social media site called *Facebook* to help users to create their own profile, upload photos, and communicate with other users... like *Steve Jobs* who gave up his university career to revolutionalise six industries: animated movies, music, phones, tablet computing, and digital publishing. *Steve Jobs* explained that a computer didn't have to be shared between four or five people in a laboratory; it could be used by just one person. His objectives were to develop a personal computer and to remove the barrier of having to learn to use a computer.

In your own life, your vision may be bigger, smaller or simpler – like being the first to develop a water bed for dogs, the first in your family to graduate from university or become a published author of a book, the first to develop a programme to help young people in foster homes to appreciate themselves and become successful, or the first to create a particular digital product or a service to impact the world around you.

Henry David Thoreau once said, *"If you have built castles in the air, your work need not be lost; that is where they should be. Now put the foundations under them."* This is a sensible mantra for consideration. For turning your vision into a reality, there has to be total dedication to the cause, and you need to act on it. This is what I refer to as a **mission**. It requires setting objectives that are specific, measurable steps to achieve what you have set out to do. These processes are called **goals**. They establish a plan for accomplishing your mission and thereby fulfilling your vision. When developing an idea, you will generally have one vision, but many goals, that is the process. Every step toward each of these goals brings you closer to realising your big vision.

This book is about appreciating who you are, what you have within, and making the most of your potential to become a creator. It reveals the practical steps in which you can generate the power, courage, hope, enthusiasm, confidence, trust and faith in yourself, to see the vision and the practical skill to make your idea vision a reality. The world within is governed by your mind, your mind is the creator of what you become or achieve. Overcome your fears, focusing on your strengths, you can find solution for every problem and discovering your gifts, and generating ideas to create financial freedom. If you are to be successful, you must lay the foundations by discovering your purpose and aspiring to live your dreams.

No matter your background, your success in the future is based on recognising your gifts and what you can create today. You can create great things if you determine to spend your time, persevering despite doubt, failure, setback, ridicule and rejection until you succeed in making something new and useful. I don't mean to make light of your present situation, but it is not your background circumstances that create the outcome of your life. Rather it is your attitudes in the present and the actions you take to control your life situations today that will determine your future success.

The basic skills you need in order to achieve your desired future are based on your ability to develop in-depth learning skills, to learn new insights from people and books, and to face life with a positive attitude.

Regardless of your circumstances, you can find the good within yourself to create **ideas** that could enhance the lives of others, to become who you want to be and get the financial riches you would like to have. Your life purpose isn't something you merely acquire. Your purpose finds you, and you know it when you create time for it and it engrosses you with such a passion that you do not think of it as 'work' or a source of stress but as a dream to achieve.

The secrets in this book offer dependable *proven* methods to maximise ideas for the benefit of young people searching to joining the league of the world's most successful people with great ideas. This is not a novel, but a practical blueprint model; it should be studied, meditated upon, and practiced to successfully develop your own innovative ideas.

Without these secrets, you might go through life as failure.

You do not need money to start. Check on "TEDx Talk" or "YouTube.com" to watch a video on any topic you want to learn about from the experts. For instance, when I started creating my online TV channel, I spent hundreds of pounds for recording and editing my videos, but one day, I reasoned within myself, and decided to do something by learning from YouTube on how to record and edit videos. Now I have a skill on how to record and edit videos, I also teach others and get paid for it. Teach yourself to discover more skills than you have now, to create your multiple stream of income. Learn anything by simply typing the keywords into the internet search box to find the topic and educate yourself; all skills are learnable. I believe that every young person is gifted with great potential; ***all you need to start is your desire to learn***. **Give yourself permission to decide to create your wealth**. Look within your areas of interest, ask questions, and take action in order to be among those whose ideas impact others' lives and who have earned financial freedom!

Note: I have provided some video links in this book to showcase some of the points discussed. It does not warrant or represent that the video will be available due to the rapidly changing nature of internet content.

Section 1: How to generate ideas

Idea is conception existing in the mind which is a result of mental understanding, awareness or activity, thought or notion as relate to you. This is a vital secret, which once contacted will set you up for a life of perpetual impact that guarantees streams of income to financial freedom. This section unveils skills, knowledge, and experience to take your ideas from conception to reality.

Chapter 1

Ten Simple Steps To Create Ideas For Invention

"Others have seen what is and asked why. I have seen what could be and asked why not" — Pablo Picasso.

Ideas rule the world in which we live now. Creating an idea for which people will pay you over and over does not take too much effort. Rather it takes strategy. However, once you have created an idea, as long as it contains relevant and up-to-date information that meet people's needs and expectations, you then have the opportunity to make money.

Creating a life of success is one thing many people wish for, but only a few take the time to achieve. Most people end up aimlessly cruising through life, hoping that one day luck or fate will make things happen for them. As I explained in my book *'You Can Be Richer Than Your Parents'* (2010), success is not accidental, but rather depends on a properly worked-out set of goals, the cultivation of an action plan and diligent adherence to this action plan. It is analysing your current situation, deciding on your main aim, and following your action plan that holds the key to utilising opportunities for producing innovative ideas. Your aspirations to achieve can propel you from where you are now to where you want to be, and take you to where you don't necessarily want to go, but ought to be. "*It is not in the stars to hold our destiny*," said William Shakespeare, "*but in ourselves*."

If you want to live a life of purpose, realising your potential and becoming the successful person you dream to be, the first thing you have to do, more than anything else, is to realise that it is only you who has the power to create the life that you have defined. You need to know what you want, which way you are heading, what you need to do. It is you who have the ability to prepare for the opportunities and remain flexible in order to overcome challenges and remove any barriers that may stand in the way of your goals and dreams. Remember that fate will not deliver your ideal lifestyle to you. But if you have the self-confidence to face your fears and see problems as opportunities in disguise, you can embrace a vision that leads to innovative ideas. The keys are optimism, faith, and a firm belief in 'greater possibilities.'

One of the most important qualities for idea-creation is the cultivation of a positive mindset for providing solutions to challenges. Wherever you go, you are bound to notice problems which can be turned into opportunities for devising an innovative idea. Everything comes to those who live fearlessly and enjoy the thrill of shaping the lives of many. Behind every successful invention is someone who saw a problem and turned it into an opportunity to come up with an idea and invent a solution or a brand-new device.

The ten simple steps for realising your ideas for innovation and invention are as follows.

- Know who you are and develop a good self-concept, believing that you can achieve whatever you set your mind to.

- Think big; think in a new dimension, with no anxieties about what could hold you back.

- Educate yourself to help you tap into the power of your potential. Knowledge enables you to explore new ways of tapping into your talent.

- Acquire basic skills on how best to take care of your mind. A healthy mind is necessary for perceiving opportunities and integrating different approaches to create an idea.

- Envision your future as creating value through creating a potentially dynamic and compelling idea that solves a problem or effects change in some area of our lives. Visualise a market that already has a high demand, seeking new solutions to some problem, in order to create an idea that can bring innovative improvement.

- Do you really want it? You must want to achieve your idea. Not because you should, but because you want to do something new.

- Take bold steps into something new that has not been invented by others before. Do something unusual and unique. Mix and match existing concepts to stretch to new horizons.

- Dream big to generate ideas that are so original and so different that they will amaze.

- Follow an action strategy step-by-step. Hope, faith and dreaming alone won't make things happen, but action can turn your idea into a reality. Act on your idea even if it doesn't make sense to others!

- Surrounding yourself with the right people and cultivating the path to accomplishing great things in your life is totally up to *you*; that is the most important thing that you need to bear in mind if you want to live a successful life.

"Great minds discuss ideas. Average minds discuss events. Small minds discuss people" – Henry Thomas Buckle.

Dick, Hansen and Nanton in '*Boom!*' (2015) stated that:

> *We have enormous problems! Better yet, we have enormous opportunities that can become omni-profitable. That's why I know in the deepest part of my soul that all of us here on planet Earth have the*

potential to enter into the biggest (positive) Boom in human history.

Imagination leads to success

"Imagination is everything. It is the preview of life's coming attractions" — Albert Einstein.

What is imagination? It is the act of forming a mental image of something not presence to the sense. It is essential to success. Many individuals struggle and have no idea of precisely where or how their life could be. This was the case for me as a failed high-school student. I was engrossed in the fear of failure, depressed, humiliated by friends, emotionally distorted, and hopelessness. I was lonely in-between crowd despite my relationship with my seven siblings, and sometimes there were strong feelings of emptiness in my life and the thought of suicide. Though, as a child, I dreamt of being a rich woman, but the shame of being a failure almost eroded my childhood dream. One day, I thought to myself, "*if it's to be, it's up to me.*" On a beautiful Saturday, I was cleaning up my mother's closet and came across my report card with my teacher's comment on my result sheet which states "*Patricia could have better grades if she pays attention in class with good attitudes and put more effort to studying.*" Suddenly I thought to myself that my dream can be achieved if I develop a positive mind-set to change my attitude, pay more attention in class, and develop good study habits.

I imagined how I could be one of the best women that could change the lives of young people in my state. I started imagining what could be done to actualise this dream, and made a shift from being in a state of despair. My imagination was focused on creating new ideas to change my study habits, be more attentive in class as stated by my teacher on my report card to improve my educational performance to achieve my desire, and eventually that worked for me.

Challenges and limitations do exist in life situations. However, the limiting beliefs only live in the mind of the pessimist, who sees the worst of everything. When you are optimistic, and use your imagination, your possibilities will become limitless. It is your imagination, as well as the positive mindset within you that guide you in the direction of achieving the goals and vision of your life. The power of your imagination makes you infinite to envision your future, and then act on your ideas like all the great achievers.

For you to be successful in life you must first think success, you must see success as attainable. Proverb 23:7 says "For as he thinketh in his heart, so is he". You are what you imagine in your heart.

Turning your challenges into great ideas

"Being challenged in life is inevitable, being defeated is optional" – Roger Crawford.

Progress is a common phenomenon that is hoped for in any business or life endeavour. It is the expectation that one walks towards – through the different stages of progression. When progress occurs, there are emotions of joy and happiness. However, when progress stalls, there are inevitably feelings of frustration and disappointment. While we are attempting to progress in the achievement of a set of objectives, there are, in fact, no guarantees that you will immediately move toward your goals, according to your well-articulated plan. Successful people are always willing to risk uncertainty in pursuit of their desires.

In developing your idea, once you have a goal and a plan in place, get going against all odds. Do something every day to move yourself forward toward your goals. Do not let the obstacles along your way discourage you.

Through going to university, working in the community and with different organisations, I encountered young people facing numerous challenges and pressures in their lives. This experience nurtured in me a strong desire and vision to help students and young people globally in a practical way, helping them develop their potential and come up with ideas to produce products or services and create their own business.

After a successful career in business, I was still frustrated by the negative impact of gang violence and gun crime among young people globally. To achieve my aim of helping young people to have aspirations, such as creating their own business, I enrolled at the University of Bedfordshire, United Kingdom in a doctoral programme in counselling psychology, focusing on the area that helped me most: personal development, self-improvement and self-empowerment.

The workload for my doctoral thesis was intense. It challenged me and took a toll on my health. Being in poor health for a while only amplified the intensity of the work I had to do, but eventually my health improved and I was more able to cope with my workload. It was about then that my burning desire to achieve my goal was severely tested in several ways.

I was late handing-in part of my course work because of my poor state of health. The progression process required that I submit my completed coursework on time. Despite strong support from my supervisory team, and the evidence of my progress thus far, the graduate school made the decision that I should not continue with my PhD programme and rather be granted the degree of Master of Philosophy and apply to start the PhD process again. While the graduate school was coming to its decision, rather than focus on the negatives and obstacles, I focused on the possibilities and the steps I could take *TODAY* to make an impact with my initial PhD research findings. And do you know what? Within just a few months, I became a famous writer, published a study habits book titled '*The Successful Student* "which reveals factors not taught in school that inhibits students from achieving better academic performance, and shows methods students can use to attain good grades without even stressing themselves, that was featured by *UK SecEd.co.uk*, and other media in the UK, now published in different countries. I have also published five books on Amazon... and I did it while continuing my PhD studies.

I'm not going to tell you it was easy... but it was amazingly "doable". With a determined mindset, I made it my sole mission in life to teach and facilitate young people in developing methods for generating ideas, and developing them with a view to turning them into products or services, and marketing them so as to generate new business. My inspired vision has become a reality in that I now speak to schools and different organisations around the world with the aim of empowering young people globally.

In your own life, it is possible to turn your challenges into opportunities by determining how you respond to the given situations. When things turn negative, develop a positive mindset, healthy degree of optimism, self-confidence and openness, along with an adventurous spirit to explore possible ways of coming out of the situation rather than being pessimistic. From my experience, if you can control your immediate response, you can change the outcome of the situations. Let me illustrate, when a singer takes a step to the stage, one degree of difference can determine whether he/she comes in under par, or sinks in the stage with fear to face the large crowd. There are three circle I discovered during my struggle for turning challenge into opportunity, which I think maybe useful for any goal achievement.

- **Accepting responsibility** believing that you are in total control of the situation, and assert a powerful influence on what need to be done. To be successful, you must take responsibility regardless of the negative circumstances.

- **Leveraging any slim glimpse opportunities**, exerting control with the least strength, have faith that you can improve with effort to move forward. The journey to idea attainment is dynamic; converting your idea to reality requires you to help others understand your vision. When things go wrong, your attitude will change to make things flow better to redirect the course of action to reach your desired goals. In the process of setback, clearly define your value proposition, leveraging your time by doing only the most important things and how you can generate good results.

- **Be flexible,** as you face setbacks in your idea creation, your inner voice or that of others may say there would be no way out. You may feel like those with a fixed mindset who think their talent can't be developed, and believe their talent alone creates success instead of making effort to developing them. But when life hands you lemon turn it into lemonade. You can develop your abilities, brain and talent by learning new ways of improving your potential for great accomplishment. Do not be too uptight with yourself; try to make the whole situation be more fun. Be patient with yourself in the process, I know most people are extremely anxious to get their desired outcome of their idea and thus start to make wrong decisions when things go wrong. Convert the new idea into innovation, re-evaluate your purpose, and reaffirm what you stand for and your desire to be successful. When you are going through this tough time, don't be ashamed to share with your close associates who could encourage you in the journey.

Essential points in creating your ideas

- **The strengths within:** Identify the talents within you, those things that you are good at, and check what you are doing now that is working out well.

- **The weakness within:** These are things you are not good at, but you can improve, or if it's a struggle you can avoid doing those things and play to your strengths instead.

- **The opportunities within:** Look inward to identify actions you can take, such as the likelihood of performing better if given a chance, and any area you might be able to develop to bring innovation –– thinking outside the box –– to accomplish your desired objectives.

In this era of technology, you are positioned with great information that enlarges the capacity of the mind which can help inspire you achieve simple and creative ideas that can launch you into the world of great exploit. Learn to draw virtues from them to enhance the quality of your reasoning. May you discover them in good time!

Your idea generation decision today

What is your take when it comes to idea generation? Ask yourself these three questions.

- What have I decided on how to generate my idea?

- If so, when should I make that decision?

- What exactly will I do?

Your Discipline Every Day

Based on the decision you have made on your idea generation. What is the discipline you will practice daily to making your idea a reality?

Transformation Action

Action is the key that will help you develop your ideas

- watch video studies on YouTube relating to your decision to help you grow

- discuss with those that can help you

- read short inspiration to help you start a habit to work with your idea

Look out for great opportunities to grow

Chapter 2:

Dreaming the seeds of your success

"I have heard that the first ingredient of success is to dream a great dream"—
John Appleman

We live in a dream world and only those with dream can make a mark with great ideas.

The strength, height, and life span of any building is determined by its foundation. Life starts with having a dream. Dreams have been responsible for some of the most creative ideas and scientific discoveries that have changed the course of human history. Without dreams, there would be no aspirations to pursue. There certainly will be no objectives to reach, you will not amount to much without dreams; your dream are the seeds for your purpose. Not having dreams is like chasing a shadow in the hope of capturing it. You need to understand exactly what you wish to do and follow that purpose. You cannot accomplish anything in life without aspirations. For these objectives to be achieved, you have to search within to discover what will lead to genuine lasting fulfillment for you. According to Myles Munroe, until a purpose is discovered, existence has no meaning, since having a purpose is the source of fulfillment.

As asserted by Munroe in his book *"In Pursuit of Purpose"* (2015, pg. 3):

> *Human beings, no matter who they are or where they live, all want to be 'successful.' This success is usually defined by the superficial rewards that are so glorified by the media: wealth, power, fame, luxury and prestige. The goal of material achievement is drilled into us from an early age. Parents urge their children to work hard so they can be 'somebody.' Schools add to the pressure by using competitive grading and by offering rewards for outstanding performances. Bookstores are loaded with manuals that instruct readers how to get to the top of their fields so they can*

accumulate power, wealth and influence, and magazines, complete with cover photos that glamorize the rich and the famous, boldly promise shortcuts to success.

This relentless pursuit of 'success' has produced some unglamorous results. Divorce and suicide rates continually climb. Violence, environmental destruction and white collar crime plague every community. Emotional depression, particularly in men and women between the ages of twenty-five and forty-four, has multiplied tenfold over the last two generations. The internal benchmarks that denote personal and corporate fulfilment *are noticeably missing from our world, and a positive sense of direction that encompasses the totality of life is obviously lacking for the majority of people."*

The desire to have or be something is a natural desire in each of us. In pursuit of wealth and fame, remember your main purpose. The mission of all humanity whether it is admitted or not, is for a life of significance through contribution to others. If you want to live a life of significance and meaning, you need the mental focus to accomplish your goals and purpose. To add value to your life, have a dream to aspire to fulfill your purpose; it is essential that you recognise the difference between aspiration and purpose.

Aspiration and Purpose

Aspiration could be explained as the ambition to achieve something, seek or a pre-defined goal. Imagine yourself becoming an actor: that's an aspiration. Your wish is to become an actor, to see yourself on television, on cinema screens and, of course, on billboards. When you desire to become something, you should also be ready to accept whatever arises along the way towards achieving that goal. You should also note that aspiration is not a one- dimensional thing. It is intangible! Aspiration does not take a particular form or direction; it spreads across several channels, just like the scent of a perfume when it is sprayed. It is not just a matter of deciding to become an actor; you also need to decide what type of acting you want to do. Do you want to be in action flicks, on Broadway or on television? You should be able to provide an answer to these questions. If all you want is to become an 'actor', then it is clear that you are just starting out because your aspiration has not yet acquired a preference or a focus. You must choose to become a specific type of actor, not just an actor. Be a marketable and relevant one. Let people see you perform in new dimensions.

Aspirations give you the courage and mental fortitude to come out victorious in all your conquests. Defeat is only temporary. Bill Bartmann aspired to become rich, and was once the 25th wealthiest American. He was inspired by *"Think and Grow Rich,"* written in 1937 by *Napoleon Hill.* Although the title appears to refer to increasing your income, Hill claimed that the philosophy of his book is for helping people to succeed in any line of work, to do and be anything they can imagine.

Bill Bartmann is one of the best rags-to-riches stories around, and he has had more than his fair share of lessons to reveal for it. In fact, he's ended up being something of a failure-to-success expert and says that one of his goals is to do for failure what Betty Ford has done for alcohol addiction. As one of eight youngsters, Bill Bartmann started with nothing. His father was a janitor and his mother a house cleaner. Bill Bartmann grew up in poverty and first saw the debt-collection business from the perspective of watching his father being hounded day and night by bill collectors. In fact, his dad died of a heart attack one night, right after a bill collector had called. After hanging around in a carnival and a gang, Bill understood that he needed a much better strategy for his life.

Bill put himself through college while working at a hog slaughterhouse. He went on to get a law degree. His law practice specialised in consumer bankruptcy. Bill later got involved in real estate, oil drilling, identifying the ideal location for drilling at the correct time. The rest, he states, was recognising the opportunity. Bill Bartmann is evidence that no matter how far down you get, you'll always have the ability to pick yourself up if you aspire to be a success. When you are determined to take steps that will help actualise your aspirations and dreams, you are leading a life of purpose.

Purpose is simply the reason for which something exists. In life, you have a proposed plan to reach out to fulfill, and a true self-analysis is what is needed to creating and determining your purpose. To live a life that is in line with what you are created to be and live purposefully daily, there is necessity to reflect inwardly how you want things to be done, knowing which path to take, and which direction will take you to the desired path you want. Many people fear there is no plan for their lives. This is because they don't know their purpose and what life purpose is about. It is very vital to know your purpose in life and what it can do for you. You are the one responsible to discover your purpose, vision for the future, plan, set goals, objectives and create the idea for what you will become. You are the one to take initiative and responsibility to make your dreams come true. Steve Maraboli said that you are put on earth to achieve your greatest selves, to live out your purpose, and do it without fear. Knowing your purpose can bring in a whole new level of passion, and joy into your life. Understanding your purpose is the compass in which you can create ideas to transit into a new path of successful career.

When you actually take steps towards achieving your idea, then you are leading a life backed up by your actions to fulfill your purpose. It is not too hard to enrich the quality of your life. You are lifeless without a purpose. All you need do is aspire to be the best you can to be to create ideas and live a purposeful life.

In life we cannot all be scientists, psychologists, academician, politicians, actors, actresses, businessmen or women, and preachers. Work to discover your own purpose and identify with it to excel.

It is important to note here that every good thing starts with one step: ***an idea.*** An idea may be defined as a vital element for establishing a solution to some problem. Many modern-day billionaires make more money for themselves and their descendants from a simple idea. Well, a few of them have in fact inherited wealth from their parents but if you take a close look at many of the world's richest people, they made their wealth without coming from a wealthy background. For example, the founder of American multinational technology company Apple Inc., Steve Jobs, was one of the world's richest men. He had an aspiration and was able to follow his purpose to develop an idea. He turned his idea into a product. This helped him to gain financial freedom for the rest of his life, donate millions to charitable causes, and earn global fame.

Every product that sells well in the market today started from a central point called an **idea**. It is not magic; it all begins with you! Creating an idea involves several phases of thought which could be visual or abstract. Thoughts are ideas that result from thinking, to create the kind of idea you want for yourself, learn to control the kind of thoughts you have, for your thoughts create your self-esteem, and idea creation.

You can create powerful ideas by simply learning from expert in your area of interest, experience in your environment, or borrow some existing concepts by integrating and applying novel ways with what you have in mind.

The decision concerning your dream today

What is your take when it comes to your dream? Ask yourself these three questions.

- What have I decided on how to develop my dream?

- If so, when should I make that decision?

- What exactly will I do?

Your Discipline Every Day

Based on the decision you have made on your dream. What is the discipline you will practice daily to make your dream become a reality?

Transformation Action

Action is the key that will help you develop your dream ideas

- watch video studies on YouTube relating to your decision to help you grow

- discuss with those that can help you

- read short inspiration to help you start a habit to work with your dream

Look out for great opportunities to grow

Chapter 3:

Why ideas are so important

"All achievement, all earned riches, have their beginning in an idea"–Napoleon Hill.

Well, if somebody would give me money to start my own business or a lucky moment in life, I could achieve something great. How often have you heard (or said) something like that? How often do people think of a brilliant idea and watch life go by, waiting for their lucky break, feeling like they're relegated to the background.

Finding out the great idea for your life shouldn't depend on

"Luck" or "fate". And regardless of how life has treated you're your take is not to give up on yourself and throw in the towel. You are not limited by your life circumstances; there is something good in that idea you have in mind.

You have hope, if you could develop deep insight into that idea you have conceived, because when ideas are nurtured, its benefit is capable in taking you from nothing and making something beautiful out of you. Your idea is vital secret, which once discovered will set you up for life of perpetual impact.

Ideas drive us, ideas rule the world. It is the inner energy that brings light to the darkest hours, when others see only problems. Ideas within you initiate opportunities and innovations to provide a solution to a problem or a brand-new device that saves time or space. The key is to find, nurture and use the spirit of ideas in a way that you may not have known existed.

Before you begin creating your own idea, it is important to understand why you want to do it and what motivates you. Some people want to develop ideas for solving problems in a niche area. Others want to add value to terms of knowledge, make money for a better future, or feel that their life has been of significance. When you know why you want to create an idea, the process of doing it becomes clearer.

Ideas enable you to advance in life. Without advancement, you remain in the same place. It was ideas that birthed the automobile and other technological innovations that eased movement from one place to another. Thinking differently brings fresh ideas, and this is the key to advancing and improving your life at the same time. Ideas are therefore important as they enable the techniques and innovations that ease and resolve many of life's problems.

Ideas are known to grow and can be regarded as seeds. So don't let that seed lie fallow in the soil of your heart. You need to water and cultivate it so that it can sprout and germinate into its fullest possible size. This could be the beginning of something that grows into the latest technological innovation globally. This image of ideas as seeds gives a basis for producing anything that matters to you in personal life or in the business world, whatever its nature.

Ideas are a driving force that cannot be ignored in our lives. In fact, society gradually changes its appearance because of ideas. We even see the spirit of sharing ideas, enabling togetherness, when it comes to creating successful products, services, solutions and the like. Thinking differently greatly impacts your personality, empowering you and enabling you to realise your power in business, relationships or in the wider society.

From the past to the present, it is through ideas that technology has advanced to where it is today. It is through ideas that we have everything from aeroplanes to light bulbs. With continuous improvements, these innovations have massively impacted the way we live and to subsequent generations. In many ways, life is not as hard as it used to be for our great grandparents. More and more processes are becoming automated, continuing to improve people's lives. Machines continue to be developed, which in turn makes work easier, both in the office and at home.

Ideas therefore need to be realised for them to have an impact. It can be better to let the mind wander so as to get that brilliant idea than to try to arrive at a solution too directly. The more you think, the better you become at connecting the elements that can form a solution or transform your views. It is recommended that you generate lots of ideas, so that you can assess which are the best while filtering out the less effective ones. No matter what kind of innovation it is, everything came to be as a result of simple ideas which were given the opportunity to grow.

In my own life situation, I had an idea to inspire students and young people in a practical way, to develop their potential, motivating them to transform their lives by developing a vision of what they want and translating that vision into reality. It was clear to me that teaching students how to study effectively and showing them how to achieve their potential would be a great benefit. I was aware that the success I was then enjoying was as a result of decisions I had made when I first started university. Little did I know then where my burning desire with the idea would lead me.

My inspired idea has become a reality in that I now share my motivational messages in schools and organisations around the world, helping to empower young people today to achieve their life dream.

Everything a person becomes is a function of the decision you made. So how do you make the necessary discovery of your ideas?

What decision have you made on the importance of your idea today?

What is your take on the importance of your idea? Ask yourself these three questions.

- What have I decided on the importance of my idea?

- If so, when did I make that decision?

- What exactly will I do?

Your Discipline Every Day

Based on the decision you have made on the importance of your ideas. What is the discipline you will practice daily to show the importance of your idea?

Transformation Action

Action is the key that will help you develop your ideas

- watch video studies on YouTube relating to your decision to help you grow

- discuss with those that can help you

- read short inspiration to help you start a habit to work with your ideas

Look out for great opportunities to grow

Chapter 4

Listening to your inner voice to create ideas

"Don't let the noise of others' opinion drown out your own inner voice" – Steve Jobs.

"Patricia you have just one more opportunity to prove you can do it" that was the echo that kept me moving forward. In my early life, everything was motivated by fear. I was driven by my fear of the realms around me, of the dream I hold dear to accomplish, of the people that interact with me on a daily basis, of the ideas I have and action needed to complete each daily task.

I was pretty much fearful of success; fear for rejection of the concept I have from my small still voice, fear from opinion of key persons in my life, and these drains me physically and emotionally to bring into reality the ideas from my inner voice.

Believe that you can. I know this works, because I'm living it myself. At one time, all I had was a dream idea. All I had was something inside of me. Around me I didn't have any parts of my dream yet, but something in me kept saying, your dream from your inner mind can be achieved if you pay attention to your inner voice. The key to attaining this is simply repeating few words of positive affirmation to yourself that you can; self talk reflects your expectation from your life and an evidence of determination in your future.

The inner voice is very powerful when it comes to meditation. Anyone who has tried to access this inner voice will find that it is always present and that it tries to communicate from time to time. Your inner voice links in with your unconscious mind and can provide important messages and answers to any life issues. When you are aware of your inner voice and thoughts you can receive answers to concerns or challenges that can help you respond more resourcefully and positively. In fact, it can guide your choices and direct you to where you need to be. Everywhere you go keep an open mind, absorb information like a sponge for ideas to get creative to do the impossible. Below are 7 methods for getting the most out of your inner voice.

7 steps to creating ideas from your inner voice

1. Exchange negative thoughts:

This is the first step to listening to your inner voice in order to come up with an idea. Learn to filter negative thoughts from your thought system. For example, *"Everything I do goes wrong"*, *"No one really loves me,"* *"I will never get anything right."* Practice exchanging all the negative thoughts that flood your mind for positive ones, which are rational and helpful. For example, *"I will meditate on what is going well in my life,"* *"Who am I getting on well with?"* *"What is not working well,* and *"what do I need to change?"* You have to think firmly that you will be able to attain the outcome that you are hoping for.

2. Redefinition:

One way to encourage your soul to think more deeply is by redefining what it means to be successful. Calmly reflect on your inner voice to discover not simply what you do, but who you are. To hear your inner voice, you need to quieten your mind, making it easier for you to listen to it. When your mind is silent, it is free from distractions. This stillness makes it possible for you to pay careful attention to the words of your heart.

3. Meditate:

This is another way of communicating with your inner voice, concentrated mental attention. Meditation is the act or process of spending time in quiet thought, to gain more insight into an idea. This will enable you to control your thoughts and let your higher self-take control until you are able to see through into a solution. You need to give mental attention to the ideas of your vision, through meditation. The more effective you are in the art of meditation, the more mentally distinct you will become. All successful people are great thinkers, great thinkers are potential inventors.

4. Be passionate:

Being passionate starts with believing in yourself. This is a burning desire, a driving force to accomplish a task; you will have the force to keep at it. Once you have it in mind that you are creative and capable of coming up with something innovative, then you are half way there. Being passionate starts within your heart. It helps you to do better and achieve your goals.

5. Focus:

Once you have identified the need for an idea, you then need to focus on this idea. Focusing is a skill which can be cultivated into a habit. Being distracted from your idea may lead you to lose direction. If you really want success, your ability to focus your mind is a critical piece of that success puzzle. Focusing is critical to elevate your thinking to the next level. Focusing starts from within and requires training yourself to listen to your heart, and getting into the momentum flow state that can't be stopped. When creating your idea, you need to be extremely careful to identify what breaks your focus. You need to develop a strategy to prevent factors that interrupt your focus. Finally, you need to practice doing one task at a suitably allocated time to be productive daily.

6. Be true to yourself:

There should be no need to deceive yourself in any way. Being true to yourself starts with listening to what the heart is trying to communicate. Ignoring the message from your heart could lead to false conclusions and acting in such a way that is not true to self.

7. Pay attention:

You should not forget to pay attention to your inner feelings. You need to be ready to receive information when you least expect it. The depth of information you have largely determines the greatness of your mind. The most effective way of information acquisition is by reading and meditation. Receiving insights does not always happen automatically, it takes practice to be able to distinguish the inner voice from all the other voices.

An inspirational teacher who conquered adversity to achieve her goals is *Gillian Thomas*. As described by a UK newspaper the "Watford Observer," Thomas had a deformity in her arm due to a medical accident when she was a baby, but she did not let this stop her from achieving her goal of becoming a teacher and achieving her dream of becoming a professional dancer too, despite being told it was not possible. She was passionate about what she wanted to be. She remained focused and true to herself. Against all odds, she listened to her inner voice, and paid attention to the feelings within.

Choice of listening to your inner voice is one of the principal factors of developing your ideas, and so must be given adequate attention. Train yourself and do all you can to nurture your mind to it, great stars in industries are those who are willing to make sacrifice to discover, and give it all it takes to get there.

Your decision to listen to your inner voice to create idea today

What is your take when it comes to listening to your inner voice? Ask yourself these three questions.

- What have I decided on how to listen to my inner voice?

- If so, when should I make that decision?

- What exactly will I do?

Your Discipline Every Day

Based on the decision you have made on listening to your inner voice. What is the discipline you will practice daily to listen to your inner voice to create ideas?

Transformation Action

Action is the key that will help you develop your ideas from your inner voice

- watch video studies on YouTube relating to your decision to help you grow

- discuss with those that can help you

- read short inspiration to help you start a habit to work with your inner voice

Look out for great opportunities to grow

Chapter 5:

The dynamics of desire for achieving end-results

"Do not spoil what you have by desiring what you have not; remember that what you have now was once among the things you only hoped for." – Epicurus

I have always had a desire to do something for others in need when I was in my teens. Somewhere in the midst of those early years, something got hold of me that I call 'desire'. Desire could be explained as longing to have something, strongly wishing for or wanting something. When you crave for, set your heart on, yearn for, desperate for or aspire to.

One way it showed was my love to inspire my peers to develop their potentials. When I was fifteen years old, I sponsored two young people in secondary school; I was involved in small business during my long summer holiday to pay their bills.

A burning desire for awakening great ideas

A number of factors nurtured in me a strong desire to help students and young people in a practical way. These factors included my personal experience as a failed high-school student, what I learned at university, and my experience of working with organisations involving working with young people in the community. My idea was to help them to avoid the negative psychological effects that I suffered as a result of my lack of vision during my early teenage years and to help them achieve their full potential.

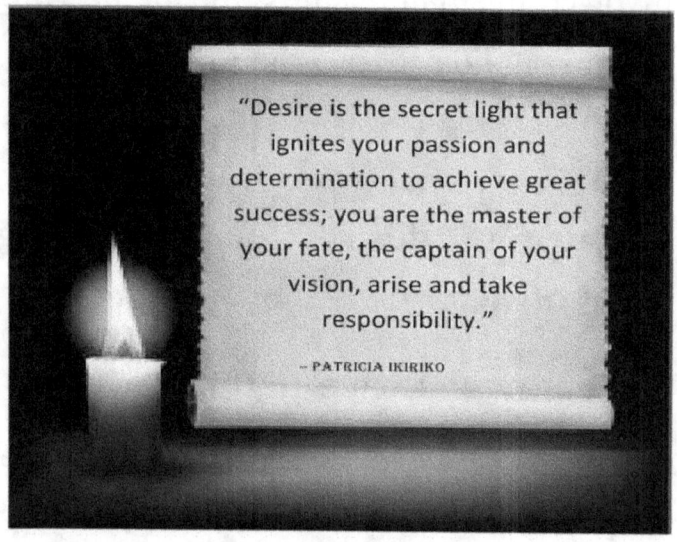

"Desire is the secret light that ignites your passion and determination to achieve great success; you are the master of your fate, the captain of your vision, arise and take responsibility."

— PATRICIA IKIRIKO

With this desire burning inside me, I have published five books all selling on

Amazon.com and a great programme titled, 'Young and Influential' A Television channel on YouTube.com, with a view to helping young people develop their potential of implementing their ideas into producing products and marketing it as well as creating their own businesses around the world. These are helping many young people to develop their potential to achieve their desired goals. Among the books, *"The Successful Student"* (2013) has been published in different countries and is used as a study habit book in some schools worldwide. This part of my goal has been achieved, and young people in Europe, America, Africa and South East Asia are benefitting from it.

The point I'm trying to make is that developing your ideas doesn't begin with your special talent; it starts with a desire to begin. You have to have the desire first or you can't do anything concrete.

See your life without limit like Louis Braille, who lost both eyes at an early age of three in an accident in his father's harness shop. He didn't let the situation discourage him from moving forward in life to make an impact, but he had a desire. His aim was to read and write, he said, I'll make a system that can help other blind people to read and write too, so he invented the system that's now named after him, the Braille system. For sure, he had a desire to do it, and he accomplished it.

Nobody wants to settle on an idea without bringing it to reality. Implementation of the idea is equally important so that the end result is something to smile about. There are many reasons why people want to see their idea develop into the desired end-product or service. It is satisfying when our efforts amount to something. The desire needs to arise from your values and motivation behind the achievement so that there is consistency in the whole process. The importances for achieving end-results are the following:

Success:

This is what most people desire when they think of the end results of creating an idea. Being successful means that everything went smoothly and you can return home with your head held high. Success also affirms that your belief in the idea was justified. It also goes hand-in-hand with social approval, power and other societal rewards.

Pride:

This is what we feel when we have actually achieved what we set out to do. It refers to the boost in self-esteem we feel when our efforts are noticed and valued. We feel recognised and important. This could also pave the way for future achievements because it is based on a motivational strategy. Being proud of yourself makes it possible to feel worthwhile.

Recognition:

A good end-result enables others to know who you are and what you are capable of doing. Being recognised can change the way you perceive yourself, and this could dramatically alter the course of your life. Those who are recognised in society may act as role models, motivating others to follow suit, inspiring them to see themselves as competent to do what they think is impossible for anyone to do. Recognition also gives you the upper hand in handling any matters arising from the end-result of your idea.

Assessing oneself:

This is a necessary activity to perform in order to know yourself better. Assessing yourself enables you to compete with yourself and lets you know how far you have come in terms of achieving your goals. It is also a way of determining whether you need to change your approach or adopt a different strategy in pursuing your objectives.

Financial Freedom:

This is to generate your multiple streams of income for your business exploit.

Being successful with your desire is all about being positive and if you think of success, this builds up self-confidence; and positive thinking is the combination which is needed in order to get the most out of your desire. Whatever you desire to achieve out of any ideas, be it in producing product, services or your personal life the key is to actually succeeding is believing in yourself and your ability to accomplish whatever it is you want to do. Thinking success leads to success, learning how to think positively is the means to learning how to think successfully and once you start to think successfully you have the power to change almost any aspect of your desire.

Many years ago, I was watching the movie titled 'woman of substance', and looking at the lead character Emma, I told myself "I can be successful". And today, I am a success writer with more than 5 books. Determination and perseverance are what is needed for desire attainment; if you don't give up on your desired idea then you can't fail. It is everyone's desire to achieve a successful end-result without hitch. This calls for consistency of values and behaviour. A conflict between values and behaviour could lead to time-wasting and a lack of productivity.

Dare to desire beyond where you are now! Stay committed to your desire, and the world that thinks you are nothing today will celebrate you tomorrow.

Your decision on your desire today

What is your take when it comes to your desire to achieve result? Ask yourself these three questions.

- What have I decided on my desire to achieve result?

- If so, when should I make that decision?

- What exactly will I do?

Your Discipline Every Day

Based on the decision you have made on your desire to achieve result, what is the discipline you will practice daily to making your desire come true?

Transformation Action

Action is the key that will help you develop your ideas

- watch video studies on YouTube relating to your decision to help you grow

- discuss with those that can help you

- read short inspiration to help you start a habit to work with your desired idea

Look out for great opportunities to grow

Chapter 6:

Developing ideas from inspiration

"It takes but one positive thought when given a chance to survive and thrive to overpower an entire army of negative thoughts," – Robert H. Schuller.

What is inspiration? I simply describe inspiration as influence moving your mental ability to receive revelation. In your quest for success inspiration is essential key that is necessary. When you received an inspiration from anywhere, you get brand new ideas which motivate you to do something innovative.

Life is a journey that begins with a single step. Similarly, every thought begins with an inspiration. This thought leads to actions which can turn out to be life-changing. It is well known that inspiration plays a big part in driving the mind. Inspiration refers to a sudden brilliant or timely idea. When it comes to developing a thought, there is a measure of inspiration that takes place before you can start putting ideas together. This is because inspiration prompts you, and the urge could come from various influences, both seen and unseen.

The process of being mentally stimulated to do something creative may be triggered by an inspiring object or image which activates the deepest recesses of your mind. Everything starts from within the mind, and ideas can only be realised by having a flexible mind. A flexible mind is one that can be molded around the object or image in order to get an exact impression of it. As long as the mind is fixed in a pre-determined direction, it might not be possible to achieve inspiration.

Inspiration is also the driving force behind imagination. Imagination enables us to explore ideas about things that are not physically present around us. It enables us to see the impossible as very possible. Through the power of the imagination people now drive their dream cars and live in their dream houses. From a flicker of the mind, inspiration makes anything possible.

Thought can also be developed from inspiration shaped by your personality. The interests and motivations that you have may act as an inspiration for you in quite a different way from those of other people. Each person has different levels of knowledge in different areas and this makes your capacity for understanding the world different as well. This means that your thoughts may guide you in a particular direction as to what inspires you in life.

Inspiration could also arise from your desires. Sometimes the only way to satisfy your desires is through your own inspiration. It may surprise you that others don't get inspired by the same things that you do. This is simply because other people may not have had the same desires as you so their mind does not respond to same sorts of stimuli as yours does.

While inspiration can be sudden, developing a thought from that inspiration is often gradual. Much of this thought depends on positive thinking. I *'CAN DO'* mentality is a vital component in nurturing your inspiration. Bear in mind that you can do whatever you put your mind to, with thoughts like, *"Yes I can do this"*, *"I will try it one more time,"* *"I can do all I want to do,"* "Nothing can stop me," *"Others have done it, so I can do it too,"* *"I have got a plan to get started and I'm going to finish it,"* *"I'm committed to confront any challenges that may come my way, and not retreat.*" It is through this kind of mindset that you can push yourself beyond what you thought you were capable of, and all in the name of inspiration.

"If you want to be a millionaire, think like a millionaire" – Anonymous.

Thought defines results. It is important that you speak only about what you want to see in your future:

- Become self-confident

- Speak like a winner

- Think like an achiever

- Act like a champion

The *Wright brothers* were aviation pioneers who started their mission with a mere thought, and invented the world's first successful aeroplane. They took action by setting the goal of designing a machine that could fly, at a time when no one thought that was possible. They turned their inspiration into a great innovation that now contributes to the comfort of humankind's travel all over the globe. You have to believe in the power of your mind to envisage what you want and create the right skills to achieve it. This also depends on your determination to focus your thoughts in the right directions, adopting a step-by-step process in order to realise your inspired idea.

Today more than it was so many years ago, idea generation is not hard because you can source ideas from diverse technology consistently and precisely that can bring unique improvement to the need of your audience. You have to find your own idea...

Capture your idea

Idea comes from inspiration, like a small still inner voice, gentle and very supple. Writing down your idea is good way of retaining it, if you don't write it down on time there is likelihood that you may lose it. Start something; Use your initiatives to develop a way of taking down every idea that comes to your mind. My friend Rachel once told me a story of how smart she thought she was, she had an idea on starting a business, had all the idea figured out in her mind on how each part should be, she mentally organised everything but didn't write them down. She said that months passed by, she didn't take any action to implement her ideas. She narrated how a friend invited her to a conference; low and behold one of the best speakers in the conference presented the exact idea she had conceived. Remember same idea is received by many people on earth almost at the same time, but only very few implement their idea. My mentor said he keeps track of his ideas by carrying a little tape recorder handy to note his idea anytime anywhere. I keep notepad in my toilet, car, living room, in my hand bags and by my bedside to write down my ideas anytime.

When developing your ideas, if you do not have anyone to inspire you, you will expire. Diligently seek and position yourself in whatever endeavour you imagine, to be connected to giants that can inspire you to greater height. You can draw inspiration from someone who has achieved greatness in whatever area of life you are aspiring to.

Your inspiration decision today

What is your take when it comes to developing ideas from inspiration? Ask yourself these three questions.

- What have I decided on how to develop idea from inspiration?

- If so, when should I make that decision?

- What exactly will I do?

Your Discipline Every Day

Based on the decision you have made on developing your idea from inspiration, what is the discipline you will practice daily with your inspiration.

Transformation Action

Action is the key that will help you develop your ideas

- watch video studies on YouTube relating to your decision to help you grow

- discuss with those that can help you

- read short inspiration to help you start a habit to work with your idea

Look out for great opportunities to grow

Chapter 7:

Generating ideas for creating products and services

"Ideas shape the course of history" – John Maynard Keynes.

Ideas are everywhere as long as you have an interest in some topic and have *thought about it at some point. From your living room to your* neighbourhood, from the office to an institution like a school or hospital, you can find a powerful idea that is worth developing. Certain factors stand out, however, as a basis for generating the ideas that can be turned into products or services; you are likely to come up with a great idea even by using the techniques listed here

Study your market:

The best way to come up with a winning idea is to study your market. Find out what the problems and frustrations of your market are. Pick a subject or an issue that people desperately need answers to and determine to provide a solution to that problem. Then, develop that idea into a product or service for that niche market.

Existing products:

Look at what is already selling well out there and give that product or service a unique twist. Follow the experts and top sellers or providers. See what's hot on *Clickbank.com*. By giving it a twist, it can become a unique new product or service. Model it rather than copy it 'word for word'. Then introduce your own innovation to it in order to improve upon what's already out in the market.

Fellow individuals:

Human beings could be seen as the basis for generating ideas and starting any project. Let's say you are in a group discussion and you are brainstorming to arrive at some solution. How many ideas would you have gathered by the end of it all? The answer is quite a large number, as long as you were engaged and committed throughout the entire process. This makes it possible for fellow individuals to contribute to your ideas which could in fact form the basis of your innovation.

Knowledge:

The knowledge you possess is another powerful means of obtaining an idea. Your idea will succeed when you are prepared with adequate information and equipped by rich knowledge about the issue. Obtaining knowledge is like revealing the innermost quantum of light within you. Anthony Robbins has grown to become a consultant to large corporations globally by the virtue of his knowledge; the capacity of his mind has enormously enlarged. Great mind are not born but is personally developed. Success is a conscious process of knowledge acquisition that individuals subscribe to. A knowledgeable person has a broader view and sees things from many different perspectives compared to someone who may not have enough knowledge on the subject. Education is vital for raising one's level of discernment, understanding. Knowledge together with considered risk-taking can take your ideas to greater heights.

Objects:

These are what you see with your own eyes. The saying goes that a picture is worth a thousand words, and this is what an object can do. It embodies details which need only be viewed or touched once in order to trigger ideas. Objects can serve as a prompt for what the mind wants to see and probably explore. Taking a walk around a garden or attending an event is a good way to trigger your thoughts and spark off a project or solution.

Routine:

Doing something in the same manner over and over again may prompt you to start seeing things differently. A routine job or action may lead to boredom in an individual, but it could equally tune the mind into thinking in a different way. So take every object and task as an opportunity to explore your world. Trying to do things differently is a good start which could trigger an idea out of the blue.

Your mind is the source that has all it takes to generate idea, but it has to be stirred. It is however your responsibility to devise, create, design how you will realise your ideas to make it count. Your dream for developing great ideas is in information. Settle down to consciously acquire relevant information for your ideas.

Your idea generation decision today

What is your take when it comes to creating products and services? Ask yourself these three questions.

- What have I decided on how to generate idea for products and services?

- If so, when should I make that decision?

- What exactly will I do?

Your Discipline Every Day

Based on the decision you have made on your idea generation for product and services, what is the discipline you will practice daily to generate your product and services?

Transformation Action

Action is the key that will help you generate your ideas

- watch video studies on YouTube relating to your decision to help you grow

- discuss with those that can help you

- read short inspiration to help you start a habit to work with your idea generation

Look out for great opportunities to grow

Chapter 8:

Enabling creativity and innovation from simple thoughts

"Innovation is the change that unlocks new value" – Jamie Notter.

In the course of my research on thought, I came up with this statement "it is your thought that creates wealth"

Reaching the point of enabling your thoughts, creativity and innovation of ideas requires a process- it takes time, persistence, and patience. In this chapter you will discover model to develop your thoughts, the importance of holding on tightly to enable your creativity and innovation of ideas, discovering how to enjoy the process even if it takes a long time that leads you through an uncharted course which requires your total commitment and determination.

In any area of your dream, having a thought in your mind is not enough. It is your creative idea and engaging a workable strategy that guarantees productivity, and in turn wealth. The secret to enabling your creativity and innovative idea is from a simple thought, and to find something you enjoy doing so much that you would be willing to do it for free. Afterwards, become so good at it that people are willing to pay you for doing it.

Creativity, if not awakened could lie dormant due to simple neglect or some daily routine that ties you down from dawn to dusk. There are many ways of bringing creativity to light, and these are usually arising from a simple thought. Thought is the process of thinking, thought is the mode of creative nature that ideas can be conceived, it is product of all attainment. The attitude of your mind automatically depends upon what you think. The secret of all achievement, power, and all possession depends upon the way you think. Thoughts are mental activities that propel the power of your mind; your thoughts determine the outcome of your life. In a way, you are constantly creating and recreating yourself. You are today the result of your past thinking, and tomorrow you will become what you are thinking today. Developing ability to co-ordinate thoughts productively for increase output for your ideas is what makes wealth.

From this, it is obvious that in order to create your ideas, products or services, thinking must be involved so that it will take form. How may this be accomplished?

This is the important point: I have put together five keys and the benefit of thought that could provide how you may develop the faith, courage, and wisdom of right thinking.

Believe in yourself: Accepting that there is a sense of creativity in you is an important step in propelling your desire and creating ideas. Believing in yourself helps you to make sense of the world around you and can empower you to enhance your thinking about progress and achieve success. Researchers have reported that our level of creativity can actually be improved in numerous ways by practice. So as long as you are trying, it is possible to summon creativity out of that thought in your mind.

Mental Exercising: Thinking is like physical exercise you undertake to keep fit, when you engage in an exercise routine, at first you have muscle pain, but the pain relaxes as you progress on the routine. So is the application of thinking through an idea. You think about an idea with difficulty at first, when you think the same thing over and over again, it becomes easier. When you continue to think about it again and again, you no longer have any fear or doubt, it becomes an automatic habit. You can no longer help thinking about the idea; as you allow yourself to be in control through your intellect; you become positive about what you are thinking. You can engage in this process by mentally determining to do so, by your own free will, intention and persistence.

Think from a different perspective: Don't put your mind in one position but try to think 'outside the box'. Creativity can be sparked from trying to solve problems with different solutions rather than the most obvious. The best way to divert your mind from fixating on the most obvious solution is to harness your thoughts to the creativity within you. Mental exercises you can do to mentally shift your thoughts include thinking how the problem may be solved from a different angle or how someone else might have solved it. It is necessary to explore whatever ideas you have one at a time to enable you to assess the best option among them.

Imagination: Your mind is your main tool in this area so make sure to use your imagination as much as possible. Drawing a picture in your mind and mentally embracing the outcome can enable you to invent a product or a service out of the blue. During the time I was writing one of my books "The Successful Student" that was featured on different media platform in UK, I gave my heart to the imagination of the success, I was mentally focused. Many people are given to rigorous hard work, but very few take time to imagine the success of the idea. Imagination is a great asset when it comes to developing your ideas.

Moment of Reflection: As mentioned above, you have the best chance of accessing your ideas during your quieter moments in life. Taking a break from the daily hassles of life could be another form of generating creativity. When you are free from distractions, you become more aware of the inner mind. Any ideas from the inner mind can find their way into your more conscious mind. It can also be helpful to have a quiet moment like this in your favourite spot, whether by the sea shore, on top of a rock or in a garden. If the place gives you pleasure and enable you to sit quietly and think, grasping creativity and inspiration is just a click away within your own mind.

Benefit of thoughts

- Thinking is a valuable critical skill that helps you analyse right evidence for your idea.

- The involvement of thinking enables creativity and innovation for great ideas.

- Thinking enhances your problem-solving abilities and a commitment to overcome your weaknesses.

- When you engage thinking, you reflect analysis and provide critical action plan.

- During the process of thinking and reflective moments, you discover important questions and problems to formulate them clearly and precisely.

- When you implement the act of thinking into your life, success becomes easier.

- Critical thinking opens your eyes to see solutions and understand that every problem is actually an opportunity for novelty of great ideas.

- Productive thinking helps you generate many alternative approaches to solving a problem, considering the least to the most important.

- Thinking helps you to discover the potential within, provide timely and solid foundation for creative thought.

- Thinking enables you to generate variety of novel and original ideas, and creating a vivid clear picture of the nature of your creativity.

Model for developing simple thoughts

- Develop simple thought on an idea
- Talk about it to others
- Bring in action, moving beyond thought and talk
- Stay committed to the end
- Bring Idea to reality -physical product

Thinking is creative, once you have an idea that works, create for yourself whatever you desire. Do not tend to develop a narrow mind about your idea on what will work or what can't be done, stick to your idea until proven right. When you employ strategic thinking, you will have a vision of the destination to be reached, and identify dangers to be avoided. If you are to make progress to enable creativity and innovation, there is a need to be determined, disciplined, focused, and courageous to develop an attitude of thinking through every decision to become successful.

The human thought is brain behind great invention, but it does not produce wealth automatically, it must be stirred up. Once you have conceived an idea, start processing it mentally, believing that there must be a key and you will definitely provide a solution in the market place that can generate your channel of wealth.

Your idea generation decision today

What is your take when it comes to your thoughts? Ask yourself these three questions.

- What have I decided on how to enable creativity and innovation from thought?

- If so, when should I make that decision?

- What exactly will I do?

Your Discipline Every Day

Based on the decision you have made on enabling creativity and innovation from thought, what is the discipline you will practice daily to enable creativity and innovation from simple thought?

Transformation Action

Action is the key that will help you develop your ideas

- watch video studies on YouTube relating to your decision to help you grow

- discuss with those that can help you

- read short inspiration to help you start a habit to work with your idea

Look out for great opportunities to grow

Chapter 9

Making your vision a reality

"The people who say you are not facing reality actually mean that you are not facing their idea of reality. Reality is above all else a variable. With a firm enough commitment, you can sometimes create a reality which did not exist before." –Margaret Halsey.

Behind everything working, there is a secret you do not know. Everything valuable has a progressive process to achievement. Ever watched the Olympics when those athletes stand on the podium to receive their gold medal; many often breakdown in tears, crying. You may wonder why? They are not crying because of that moment of getting the medal; they remember the process they had to go through to get there: the pain, sleepless nights, the blisters they endured, the torn ligaments, the difficult times of illness when they couldn't get out like their colleagues for training. They don't consider the moment but thinking about the journey that has brought them there. That is what it takes to making your vision a reality. Making your vision a reality requires wisdom to keep standing on the knowledge every step of the way, to know that the journey is more important than the destination to become what you would never have become without it.

Visions and dreams are not just for people with exceptional talent like the genius, but for people like **YOU and I**. The process of developing your vision will break you, strengthen to make you bold, in the same way equip you to stand before great men in life.

Having a vision does not really mean that it will be realised easily as many people would desire, but it's achievable. As Julian Baggini stated:

> *"The optimist underestimates how difficult it is to achieve real change, believing that anything is possible and it's possible now. Only by confronting head-on the reality that*

all progress is going to be obstructed by vested interests and corrupted by human venality can we create realistic programmes that actually have a chance of success."

I have come to terms that no successful person succeeds by accident. A life of success is not by luck. Hard work is the secret that makes vision a reality. If you must maximise your vision, you must work hard! I purposed never to be lazy to look to others or government for assistance for my basic needs in life. I know as I determine to focus on the work at hand, I will make my vision a reality. So, I give myself to my job, celebrating the dignity in labour.

In any endeavour, dealing with the change of making your vision a reality could be daunting. However, the following tips are the ingredients for managing your vision and making it into reality.

Put it on paper:

Define your vision by writing it down. This is because once it is on paper, it can be taken more seriously than when it is still in your imagination. The moment you start drafting it on paper, many other ideas may appear and this could speed up the reality you are seeking.

Draft the strategy:

Map out the methods you need to use to achieve your idea, as this is the only way to fulfill that vision. Both short- and long-term goals should be specified so that you know what you need to tackle ahead of time. Guiding protocols should also be stated in the plan as you will need to adhere to these once your vision becomes a reality.

Break down the plan:

Are you able to eat a whole pie without cutting it into smaller pieces? Even if you take the biggest bite ever, it will still be broken into smaller pieces through chewing. This is what happens to your set plan as well. The plan must be broken down into smaller goals which are then dealt with one at a time. It is important to draw up a timeline so that everything falls into place at the expected time and date. Let the idea simmer in the back of your head day and night. Pay more attention to your thinking and meditation, make note of them all.

Evaluate the process:

Once you kick off, there should be no turning back. The only means to judge reality is to assess the successes and the failures encountered. If the merits outweigh the demerits, then you know that you have come closer to achieving your goal.

Above all, managing your vision and leading the invention transition to reality depends on your ability to focus. With a motivated focused mindset, you can withstand all odds. You should not contemplate failure or think of giving up. What should stand out are the goals and the positive risks you are willing to take. The dynamics that can determine the outcome of any change effort in making your vision become a reality is of great importance. It is your own choice in realising your vision; it's your actions that will determine the outcome of your ideas.

A well-structured plan will help you to stay motivated and on track. On the other hand, you can ask yourself a few questions to get started on positive note to generate ideas.

- What are your expectations in life?

- Are your ideas reasonable?

- Will you apply effort to reach your goals?

- What effort are you willing to put in to make your dream come alive?

- Are you prepared for setbacks?

- Do you have plans to overcome the setbacks?

- Do you understand the consequences of your efforts, aspirations, desires, intentions and vision?

Productivity is never an accident. Success is always the result of a commitment to excellence, intelligent planning, focused effort to set objectives and using great professionals with strong witty invention to navigate the curve to success.

Expert You Need

I know how it can appear daunting when you have your ideas all figured out but don't know how to fix it to create it into reality. Living the dream to cleverly extracting your uniqueness, unlimited ideas extracted from your personal intelligence, and from your innate instinct – the abilities that are not only found in your educational qualifications. Those years experience of knowledge, experience and expertise to generate ideas isn't easy. Discovering to make most of your potential takes years of success and failure to learn, determination, tenacity, diligence, self-confidence and right association.

The choices you make now and the people you surround yourself with all have the potential to affect your idea creation. The actualization of your great ideas requires working with experts who knows simple steps systems to design and create your ultimate system. How simple and 'doable' creating your knowledge can be when you have someone (who's been there) to show you how to make most of your potentials.

Franklin illustrates the help of expert to making idea a reality in his book "Believe That You Can" (2008, pg. 154):

"Walt Disney had a dream of building an extravagant faily theme park in California. He figured out that if Fowler could successfully handle everything he had done in the

military, he would have the know –how to head up the design and construction of the park, which he wanted to call Disneyland. Fowler felt he was up to the challenge, and he accepted the job. Not only did Fowler head the design and construction process, but he also managed the park's operation for years after Disneyland opened in 1955.

A decade later, Disney had a new dream-to build a similar theme park on the other side of United States, in Florida. He wanted to call it Walt Disney World, and he persuaded his friend Joe Fowler to be in charge of designing and constructing that one too. The Florida project came with even more challenges, not the least of which was creating the park in the midst of thousands of acres of swampland. By now, Fowler was seventy-one, and most people his age were taking it easy. But he said yes again. By the time it was finished in 1971, he was seventy-seven. Now he could retire.

But when he was eighty-seven years old, his friend Disney asked him to help with the design of the new Epcot park next to Walt Disney World. At eighty-seven? They had to persuade him harder this time. They flew him down to the site, and they showed him this new mission. Nobody has ever seen such a thing before, and they wanted him to build it. The fire lit up his eyes, he said yes again. Around that time, somebody interviewed him and asked, why in the world at eighty-seven would you take such a huge project on?

Fowler reply? "You don't have to die until you want to" He completed the Epcot project with time to spare"

It is important to note that success is achieved through strategic planning and empowerment, which refers to seeking out extra knowledge of skilled team with the ability and fire in their bone like Mr Fowler to do the best they can. Many of you know about success, many even desire it, but many never attain it because of their unwillingness to discover who they are and what they have within to working with the right people to achieve success.

If you want to break barriers and establish territories to make a difference with your idea, you need to realise that breakout comes before your breakthrough. You need to start by breaking out in your own mind, and into self confidence. Once you perceive the world in new ways, to find hidden patterns, to make connections between solving problems, this results in innovative approaches that pave the way to making your vision a reality.

Your decision on vision today

What is your take when it comes to making your vision a reality? Ask yourself these three questions.

- What have I decided on making my vision a reality?

- If so, when should I make that decision?

- What exactly will I do?

Your Discipline Every Day

Based on the decision you have made on making your vision a reality, what is the discipline you will practice daily to making your vision a reality?

Transformation Action

Action is the key that will help you develop your vision into reality

- watch video studies on YouTube relating to your decision to help you grow

- discuss with those that can help you

- read short inspiration to help you start a habit to work with your vision

Look out for great opportunities to grow

Chapter 10:

Developing resilience and strategy to overcome limitation

"A pessimist sees the difficulty in every opportunity; an optimist sees the opportunity in every difficulty." – Winston Churchill.

What do you do when all hope seem lost; when your world does not look like what you have anticipated, your present situation doesn't look like the vision you have set out?

20 years ago I was struggling, seriously struggling to generate ideas that work; I

determined to make a difference in the lives of young people to develop their potentials. During my teenage years struggle, I vowed that should I succeed in life, I would help other young people do the same.

I kept my promise- After a successful business career with my husband; I decided to study for research PhD in United Kingdom, in counselling psychology to focus on the area that helped me most: personal development and self-improvement, to gain more insight on research study with young people.

To my delight I found a good University in the United Kingdom. However, the opposite was true to my vision; the workload for my doctoral thesis at the University was intense. It challenged me, and took a toll on my health. Being in poor health for a while only amplified the intensity of the work I had to do, but eventually my health improved and I was more able to cope with my workload. It was about then that my burning desire to achieve my goal was severely tested in several ways.

I was late handing in part of my course work because of my poor state of health. The progression process required my completed coursework to be handed in on time. Despite strong support from my supervisory team, and the evidence of my work and progress thus far, the graduate school decided I should not continue with my PhD programme. Finally, the graduate school made a decision to grant me the degree of Master of Philosophy and ask for a new application to start the PhD process again with them. My hopes were built up again only for them to be dashed when the university rejected the application they encouraged me to make.

Also about that time my student visa expired and, as I had not got another approved course lined up to follow it, the trials included the trauma of the UK's Home Office wanting my children and I to leave the country as required by the terms of my visa. The dilemma has broken my compass, and I don't know where to go, I was confused. Hindrance can get in front of you and block you, keeping you from making progress. It hits you, trying to slow you down and trip you up to hinder your accelerated achievement. However, with firm confidence and faith in what you believe, say to yourself, this situation, you cannot stop me, you can knock me down but I will arise to achieve my set vision.

Despite these setbacks, I firmly believed that my situation would improve, and eventually it did. Today I am one of the most innovative and inspirational experts. I continue to expand my horizons, even though the challenging obstacles with today's young people and the economy. Because of my tenacity and absolute confidence in what I teach, I'm named one of the only handfuls of women who can claim to be "skilled" when it comes to inspiring young people to develop their hidden potentials to create wealth.

I now share around the world in schools and different organisations involving young people, accelerate the conversation about generating ideas into producing product, sharing how to not just survive but thrive through strategic marketing to create their business to succeed, and has helped many young people move closer to their goals of successful life and better future.

Indecision is the root of frustration, stagnation, devastation but overcoming challenge to get to any destination begins with decision. It is your decision to move beyond setback that birth greatness. In an effort to change any idea into reality, setbacks may arise but this does not mean that you are a failure. Possessing resilience will enable you to adapt to any situation while accepting any kind of feedback. What matters here is how to deal with that situation at that moment and what to do later on to avert further crisis.

Developing resilience starts from within your mind. The moment you start having an idea in mind, you need to make allowance for change and accept both positive and negative outcomes. Any difficulties experienced during the process should be viewed as strengthening steps and as challenges needed to keep the ball rolling. Take these stumbling blocks as the best teacher ever to grow and improve on those mistakes that lead to such difficulties.

In order to have a more resilient attitude, you need to be committed and show that you value what you do. Once you are committed to making your ideas a reality, then drawbacks can never thwart your efforts. It is very important to set a goal and make sure that nothing interferes with your plans. Be realistic in your strategy and follow them to the letter such that there is no breaking point or turning back. Having this driving force may require a lot of energy but it will surely be rewarded in the end.

Having confidence in yourself is another way to develop resilience. Once you believe you can do it, you then need to do it no matter what hindrances you encounter along the way. Fear is a strong catalyst for powerlessness and this is what you should work vehemently against. The slightest sense of fear will make you feel helpless and deter you from moving forward.

Decisiveness is an attitude to cultivate to develop resilience, but if you are not careful the string of limitation will get hold of your life, and suddenly you will begin to accept those limitations. You must determine to push down those limitations. Any limitations should be seen as temporary: sooner or later they will pass. If you perceive them as permanent, you are doomed. Forging ahead in times of drawbacks and discouragement, and focusing on those areas where you can move forward is far better. Avoid interfering with other areas just because one part of your plan didn't work as desired. Rather, put in more effort in those areas you are best at, so that you can maximise your results and dilute the limitations in other areas. The important issue here is to see a brighter tomorrow and enable success in the future; avoid dwelling on setback, past failure and today's limitations. Develop a positive mindset to power on against all odds.

Your decision to develop resilience and strategy to overcome limitation today

What is your take when it comes to developing resilience and strategy to overcome limitation? Ask yourself these three questions.

- What have I decided on how to overcome limitation?

- If so, when should I make that decision?

- What exactly will I do?

Your Discipline Every Day

Based on the decision you have made on developing resilience and strategy to overcome limitation, what is the discipline you will practice daily to overcome limitation?

Transformation Action

Action is the key that will help you develop your ideas

- watch video studies on YouTube relating to your decision to help you grow

- discuss with those that can help you

- read short inspiration to help you start a habit to develop resilience

Look out for great opportunities to grow

Chapter 11:

Sourcing and developing the content

"You can make positive deposits in your own economy every day by reading and listening to powerful, positive, life-changing content and by associating with encouraging and hope-building people."– Zig Ziglar.

One of the biggest revolutions online at the moment is sourcing materials for ideas. With the wide availability of high speed broadband connections globally, it has become easy for people to access materials online to develop ideas worth millions.

Sourcing is the basis, aimed at finding. Searching and keep searching until you find what you are seeking to establish. When you source the content, outlining your material make it easier for you to create your ideas quickly and easily. Content is the useful information that conveys the relevant background value to knowledge of ideas. In developing your idea, it is pertinent to be action-driven on what you do to source your content. To be completely engrossed in the things you pursue to reach the goal matters. Be patience, you might learn something to reach there that contributes to uniqueness of your idea.

Sourcing and developing an idea to its full potential needs a little push and this can come from simply believing in your ability and gathering enough courage to take up the task for sourcing your content. Excellent ideas crop up every day in your mind. Get your idea model clearly in your mind's eyes, picture it, visualise it and work daily to actualise it. Give that model to your subconscious mind to build upon – in a short time, that model will become a reality. Below are some preconditions to sourcing and developing content for your idea.

Ways of sourcing content for your idea

Your own knowledge – Personal knowledge on a subject is critical for helping in sourcing the contents of your idea and saving you a lot of time. Your thoughts can be a good source for ideas, since what comes from within is said to be powerful. Ideas can also be easily gathered from your environment. Taking inspiration from everyone around you can increase the number of ideas you have and enhance your potential to capitalise on your ideas. Developing such brilliant ideas starts from embracing and developing them, rather than dismissing or neglecting them.

There are several ways of sourcing content for your idea. One way is to look for content that is already selling in your niche and get ideas from that. You can do this by using different market places such as the following websites.

Clickbank – Have a look at product/affiliate marketplaces where you can buy popular products. Study how the content is structured in order to make up your own innovative ideas.

Google search –By entering your keywords into this web search engine, you can search specific sites. This simple but rapid method of obtaining information should not be overlooked in your quest to develop and enrich your content.

Copernic 2000– This is a free software programme that searches multiple search engines simultaneously to find what you're looking for.

http://www.copernic.com/

DataGrabber– This tool targets hundreds of public databases to dig up information.

http://www.wildcowpublishing.com/data grab.html

Deja.com – This site allows you to search lots of UseNet newsgroups simultaneously.

http://deja.com

Forum One – For searching through forums and message boards.

http://forumone.com

Encyclopedia.com – This site allows you to search through a massive database of articles, at no charge.

http://www.encyclopedia.com/

NewsDirectory.com – Look at hundreds of newspaper articles from all over the world.

http://www.newsdirectory.com/news/press/

Sign up to other vendors – Look at different lists in your niche and see what they are saying. You can even search blog posts on your topic of interest to seek out their winning points. Go through different sales pages and decide if you can create a similar but more beneficial idea.

Visualisation is very important if you keep in mind that there is no formula for thinking, no right or wrong. Every thought is actually accounted for from the very moment you start making a positive move. Don't be anxious about starting small, because a thousand miles also begins with a single step. Have faith that everything has its time and place, and this includes your ideas. Plant it in your views and give it time to grow so that one day you will see its fruits.

Developing the contents of your ideas will also depend on what you want to achieve with regards to your ideas. In this respect, it is important to assess whether you have realistic goals which are ultimately achievable. With this in mind, it is possible to determine whether you are able to make a move. It is at this point that your ideas need to shift from up-in-the-air to implementation. Make implementation a serious step and try not to lose any of your ideas. If possible, use mind-mapping software to help you to see your ideas from a different perspective.

Mindmapping

Example: Notation map

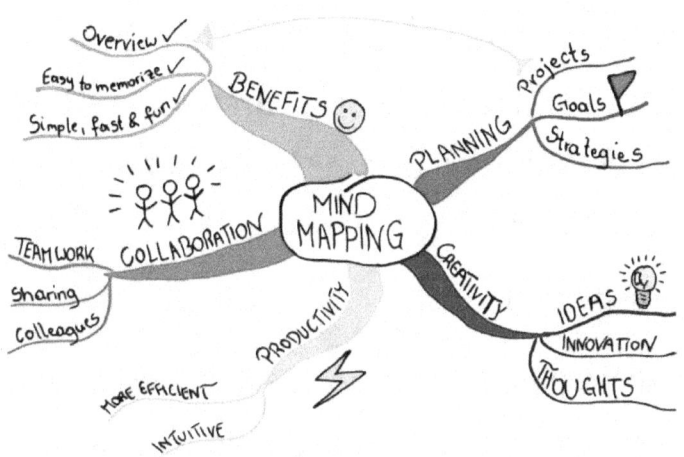

Constantly review your ideas to determine what is most important for developing your content, so you would not forget what you have done so far. Knowing and understanding what you already have makes it easy to connect to what you don't have. Obtaining an idea is a crucial step, although developing it should be the driving force behind it. You need to give a lot of thought as to how you will implement the idea so that your dream is achieved. Do not let your dreams lie fallow beneath the soil of your heart, but let them sprout and nurture them so that they turn into a reality.

Creating ideas is a very inspiring event and even more so if you are able to live your dream and attain the desired output. No matter what kind of ideas you have, know that it is very possible to turn it into the riches of your life as long as there is focus, determination and a willingness to innovate, doing something different from all the rest.

Ways of preparing your content ideas to be accepted

When working on your content, consider how you could make your idea more inspiring for your niche. Nothing matters more when creating your idea than the people you intend to serve. The more they feel like you are offering them something special, the farther your idea will go.

Accelerating change and selling your idea are major keys to consider when planning your idea. Regardless of how open-minded people are, they tend to be biased against new ideas. Paradoxically, you can enable acceptance of your innovation by expecting resistance to your new idea and planning for it from start. Crafting your pitch so as to maximise certainty will alleviate any doubts and uncertainties that your audience feels, enabling them to recognise the idea as truly novel and useful.

When creating an idea, it's not only the creative and artistic expression that will make your idea acceptable in the market place, but also the presentation of its purpose. Great ideas are accepted depending on how the story is sold. The title of your idea will attract people's attention, but it's the structure of the story that will retain your idea in their minds. By clearly conveying the purpose of your product or service, you will be able to get the attention, interest, and desire of customers. With an articulate, structured advertisement affirming the features and benefits of your idea, you can persuade customers to accept your idea. Statistics shows that advertisements can make people more susceptible to impulse buying. Personally, good advertisements make me gullible enough to buy things that are not on my shopping list, particularly nice shoes, bags and dresses. My husband often says that I rationalise my purchases by thinking that the new bag will go with a particular dress in my wardrobe!

Making your idea authentic

Make your idea believable. Create unique packaging and labeling that is brief, powerful and compelling. Show the benefits of your idea through storytelling. Quantify all your claims to make your idea stand out from the rest in your niche. Use psychological triggers to attract interest.

Consider the following:

- Who is the idea for? Who is your target audience?

- What benefits will others derive from your idea?

- Why should they care about your idea? Thoroughly explain this part in detail. There are many ideas around like yours. Some are of high- quality. Describe a general problem you know people in your niche have encountered, and then provide details about the solution that your idea will offer – *"what's in it for me?"* Stipulate the problem which your idea solves. Write or film a compelling message about the benefits. Use bullet points such that each point engages the readers, making them curious and excited about what your product or service can do. Stipulate clearly what makes it different.

• Offer a solution in such a way that it makes your audience think *"Yes, that's exactly what I'm looking for to solve my problem."* To point out the benefits of your idea, think of it as similar to telling a story relating a problem and a solution. This will help to engage your audience and leave them feeling an emotional connection.

- Highlight why your audience should desire your product or service, since activating their interest will prompt them to take action.

Model experts' ideas in your niche

Watch what the experts in your niche are doing and how they are doing it. Model their ideas but bring something unique to the existing product or service. Apply your own innovation to existing ideas and use the knowledge they share to make your own ideas stand out.

Your decision to sourcing and developing content today

What is your take when it comes to sourcing and developing content? Ask yourself these three questions.

- What have I decided on how to source and develop my content?

- If so, when should I make that decision?

- What exactly will I do?

Your Discipline Every Day

Based on the decision you have made on sourcing and developing content, what is the discipline you will practice daily to sourcing and developing content?

Transformation Action

Action is the key that will help you develop your ideas

- watch video studies on YouTube relating to your decision to help you grow

- discuss with those that can help you

- read short inspiration to help you start a habit to develop content for your idea

Look out for great opportunities to grow

Section 2: Maximising your success

Success is the price for winners, but the actualization of it is your own responsibility.

This section explores the factors that motivate all positive changes, decisions, and choice for taking control of your life to unleashing your incredible potential that make up for personal success to developing multimillion ideas.

Chapter 12:

How do you make most of your potential?

Power Within

"Successful people maintain a positive focus in life no matter what is going on around them. They stay focused on their past successes rather than their past failures, and on the next action steps they need to take to get them closer to the fulfillment of their goals rather than all the other distractions that life presents to them." – Jack Canfield.

How do you make most of your potential?

Everyone is born a leader. To lead in providing solutions to the problem you are created to solve. Your background, race, and looks do not matter. People are more interested in what you can do to alleviate their plights or solve their problem.

Inside you lay the seed of greatness and the ability to become what you were created to be; just as in every seed is a tree. The seed may not look anything like a tree until it undergoes a long process of growth. Only then does it become a tree. The seed needs to be planted in the soil, and nurtured and nourished until it pushes through the soil to receive sunlight. This will enable it to grow and eventually bear fruit. So it is, with each individual. To become what you were created to become, you need to nurture yourself in the right environment; learn from books, media, and relationships so as to discover your gift. You have been created to function effectively in a position of leadership, to develop ideas, produce products and services, create your business, and realise your dreams of becoming a success.

From my experience of working with young people for over 18 years and from research I conducted as part of my doctorial study between 2009 and 2013 (on the effects of counselling on the study habits and locus of control of senior secondary students) and from engaging in practical and analytical counselling work with the students, I was able to draw conclusions about why many young people do not do as well academically as they could. It is not simply the teaching methods or study techniques that affect a student's academic outcomes; rather there may be hidden psychological blocks which impede the person's trajectory path towards success. These negative factors must be identified before an individual can achieve success.

The journey starts from the discovery of 'who' you are and the true acknowledgement of 'what' you have within you, so that you can be 'what' you want to be, thus, the **innovation of trajectory** for personal success to develop the seed 'talent' embedded in you.

What is a trajectory?

Before we begin, it is pertinent to be very clear about what I mean by trajectory, since there are several meanings of the word 'trajectory'. Trajectory could be explained as the path or course of a given system at a constant angle; a progressive pattern of change and development that leads to a result. Some of the synonyms of 'trajectory' include: path – curve – route – direction – flight – flow – movement – range – track – trail.

It can be seen that there are three meanings of the word 'trajectory'. One has to do with **path**, another has to do with **constant progression** and the other has to do with **the result**. These concepts are important to explore since we all have a desire to be someone or to achieve something. The journey to life success starts from the discovery of 'who' you are and acknowledgement of 'what' you have within you, to live life consciously so that you can be 'what' you want to be. Work with passion to speed up your success, for time waits for no one.

Many young people today are living without a purpose. They just meander through life without any aim and without actualising their real potential. They have no idea of 'who' they are; they do not even know 'why' they exist. They do not understand anything about the 'what', 'where', 'when' and 'whom' of their existence; and have no vision for their future. Because of this, they never really get to discover the value embedded within them.

Many do not even know what gifts they carry; some know, but are at a loss as to how to harness that divine-given potential. Others are plagued by the fear of rejection or some other phobia; while yet others permit their life situation and circumstances to distort their views and stop them from aiming higher. This prevents them from developing and fulfilling their dreams.

My Trajectory Model

Patricia Ikiriko's Trajectory Model for Personal Success

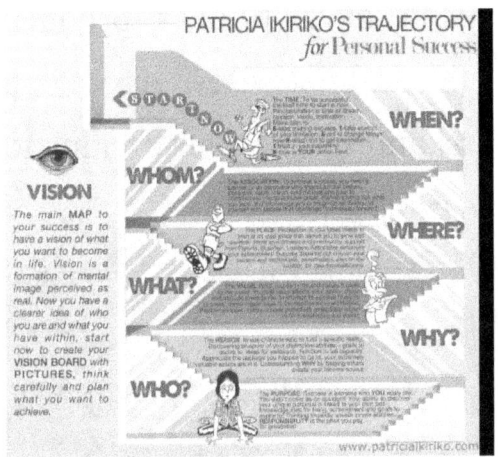

This **trajectory model** is a detailed, graduated **process** to help you understand that:

- You were created special in your own way, fitted with everything needed to discover and harness your true potential;

- You have all it takes to become the great '**You**' you wish to become;

- You also have all it takes to design your vision, develop ideas, produce products and services, create a business, and realise your dreams to become a success!

1. WHO?

This refers to your **PURPOSE**. You are special! You are one rare work of genius! No one else on earth is exactly like you. You were created with a mission, a PURPOSE. You are not an accident! You were exclusively created to achieve a divine purpose. No matter how hard others try, they cannot fulfil your destiny, only you can! You are so different from everyone else. Hold onto your image. Your ability to discover your unique potential is linked to your own self-knowledge. Knowing who you are makes a difference in how you live your life. It is important to know your identity as this enables you to be very clear about your uniqueness. If you don't know your identity, you will be denied many things. Knowing who you are will help you identify what you are qualified for and what you can do. People commit suicide on a daily basis because they know little about themselves; they have no idea who they really are. The picture you have of who you are will determine how others treat you. Who you are, determines your action, and what you can achieve in life.

The hardships you confront may be quite depressing, and this may cause you to lose focus in life and get into a rut. Do everything you can to explore ways of getting out of this rut. Coming out of this rut is very important for your personal growth and life achievement. Do not be afraid of anyone taking your power concerning who you are and what you can do. Responsibility is the price you pay for your greatness. It doesn't matter what circumstances are surrounding you at any given time, you must always see yourself in a positive light, as worthy. Every morning when you rise, confidently know that you are a victor and not a victim; there is much more to yourself than you can see.

If you have a limited perception of yourself, you will be convinced that you have no purpose, power or potential, and that your background means you won't amount to anything. Sometimes you may be reminded of all the disappointments you've endured, and you may end up with self-doubt and low self-esteem.

You are the solution to a particular problem! Yes YOU!

Note: Check on TEDx Talk or YouTube.com to watch videos on topics relating on 'who you are'.

Enjoy this videohttp://bit.ly/23axnxK (Mana: The power in knowing who you are | Tame Iti | TEDxAuckland) if the link is available to watch!

Know and accept that you are indeed unique, and strive to discover by all means who you really are. And when you do, embrace it with courage and move on.

A good example is a man born without limbs. His name is *Nick Vujicic*. He was formed the way he was to fulfil a purpose. Now, you might wonder, "*What sort of purpose can a limbless individual possibly fulfil?*" Well, he was created to fulfil a special purpose of restoring hope to many people on the earth! Just as Nick swiftly realised that his disability wasn't a curse, but rather a feature of his unique purpose, so you can also go on to discover your own uniqueness and potential. Understand that fate has installed in you certain gifts peculiar only to yourself. It is the use of this gift that will make your world wonder at what you will become!

You are uniquely designed to be you. You are appointed to solve a particular problem on earth. A lot of people are waiting for you to provide the solution, and you might be able to meet their needs. There are many things that will not get into shape until you accept who you are and what you have within. There are a lot of people whose lives are attached to your purpose, so if you do not manifest your uniqueness you will not be able to enrich or ease their lives. Until you shine, other people may not be able to shine. That is why it's important to know who you are. Discover your potential to make a difference. This generation has an expectation of you and it is waiting for you. Having a clear intention helps you to create the outcome you want. When you acknowledge who you are, and set your daily personal goals, your life will take a new turn.

Your future is in the difference you can make.

Note: Check on TEDx Talk or YouTube.com to watch videos on topics relating to 'the power of attitude'.

Enjoy this video http://bit.ly/ZaLnOk (Nick Vujicic - Attitude is Altitude.com / Life Without Limbs.org) if the link is available to watch!

"Souls who follow their hearts thrive; fools bent on evil despise matters of soul" — Proverbs 13:19-25.

2. WHY?

This refers to the **REASON** underpinning what you are doing. The package you happen to be in has a reason. You were specially created to fulfill a specific purpose on the earth. Your body structure, your looks and every notable characteristic about you are all divine installments in you to help you fulfill that purpose. A wonderful plan has been designed for you, and that is why you have been created to be tall or short, or light-complexioned or dark-complexioned. You are the only one who can manifest the innate potential within you. Recall that great blessings often come in small packages. Embrace who you are! Determine against all odds to identify your uniqueness. This will help you to pass through the various stages to envision a blueprint of what you desire for a great future.

A healthy adult male can release between 40 million and 1.2 billion sperm cells but it only takes one sperm and one egg to meet and create a baby. Among the 1.2 billion sperm cells present during fertilization, you were the only one to survive. Your life is important. You have been given a chance to choose your why. You have only one life, so live it to the full. The knowledge of your existence is the manifestation of your potential, based your mindset of what is within you that you love to do.

Your *WHY* is to help someone to get their hands on something they want, solve their problem, or avoid something painful in their life. In order to be successful, you need to appreciate what you have despite your limited resources, and do what you have an aptitude to do. Accepting your *WHY* will produce your business and your channel of wealth. In addition, accepting this *WHY* will drive you to achieve more, help you stay committed, and helps you to accurately interpret your circumstances and get the best out of them. You can acquire great riches once you realise your "*WHY*!"

There is the story of a lady whose parents were very wealthy, she spent money lavishly living an extravagant life in New York. Her parents sent her a special package wrapped in some unattractive paper, from their base in another country. Upon receiving it, this lady abandoned the gift in her wardrobe without bothering to open it, assuming it wasn't worth anything. One week later, she lost her parents in an aeroplane crash. This prompted her to start auctioning off some of her properties to pay her huge bills as well as her mortgage. Before long, she became bankrupt. Unable to pay the mortgage on her house, she eventually lost her house to the bank. Two decades on, the once classy lady was now living in a slum with beggars! She scarcely had enough food to eat. One fateful day, she stumbled upon an old box in her wardrobe, and lo and behold there was the old, unattractive paper-wrapped gift she received from her parents. Nonchalantly, she opened it – only to find a document containing the details of her parents' investments on her behalf! These enabled her to move out of poverty and live comfortably again.

Moral lesson

- Do not ignore the package you happen to be in; your extremely valuable assets are inside it.

- Do not allow temptations around you to distract you from your mission.

- Understanding your WHY will produce your source of income in terms of a business.

You can become a great model in any form you're born with.

Note: Check on TEDx Talk or YouTube.com to watch videos on topics relating to the reason for your personality, and breaking down barriers.

Enjoy this video http://bit.ly/1YVWtPL (Down's syndrome model Madeline Stuart stars in romantic fairytale wedding photoshoot) if the link is available to watch!

3. WHAT?

This refers to **VALUE**. The main value for which you were made is to bring about a change in your generation. However, you must cultivate a positive mindset in order to be clear and make wise decisions. A positive mindset is also needed to successfully unravel the potential within you, no matter how limited, so as to achieve your purpose on earth. The value you have of yourself will have a significant effect on your ability to facilitate your performance. It also determines your attitude towards life, what you envision for yourself, and what you see. Having a clear perception of your self-value will surely help you to birth an appropriate vision, and also to strategise and prioritise targets. It will be through your action, character, and attitudes and self-value that you will determine who comes to you and how you can tap into your talent. You are the only person who has authority over your own value; this is why value is at the top of the personal-development trajectory. To be authentic with high self-esteem, you need to genuinely care about yourself and be clear of your personal value, since everything else flows from it. Your value is in the problems you are willing to solve, which creates the wealth and the business value which you deliver to the world.

Your potential can be a kind of educational programme in that if you believe in it and feel it is very important for people, you can offer help to others. Your potential skill is the information that can help someone become a master at what they want to achieve. No matter how small you think your potential talent is, strive to be the best at your core value. Become conscious of all the good things about it, and just do what you can. Whatever you focus on will expand and increase, so let everything in your environment teach you and bring out the best in you. The picture you portray of what you do with your potential skill shapes how others treat you and what you can achieve. According to Robert Shuller in his book *"If It's Going to Be, it's up to Me: The Eight Proven Principles of Possibility Thinking"* you need to develop your skills yourself, so you have something to offer others, since no one else is going to work on it for you. Think of your little potential as the great idea that is going to change lives in the world and really believe in it.

Have a positive mindset about what you love to do and make a firm decision to embrace your unique ability. Stick to your goals with confidence. Create a story about why you are the best person for that idea. Do the work that needs to be done to build up your body of work. Use every opportunity that comes your way, as you never know which will yield success for you.

Let these ideas be so real in your mind that they push you to do whatever you need to. Discover what you are passionate about in order to attain success.

A good example is *"The Gifted Hands"* about Dr Ben Carson who becomes a world-class paediatric neurosurgeon at the prestigious Johns Hopkins Hospital. When he was a boy of about 11 years old, Ben Carson was failing school. His single mother, who had but a third-grade education, was distressed about her son's academic failures. She decided to do something about it. She set him two books to read per week and required that he write book reports. Ben and his older brother Curtis soon begin to love reading and learnt many things from the world of books, so that within one year Ben went from being at the bottom of his class to the top.

Clarity on your *"WHAT"* can guarantee you financial independence and a great future.

Your value within matters!!!

Note: Check on TEDx Talk or YouTube.com to watch videos on topics relating to motivation, value, and your 'what' for existence.

Enjoy this video http://bit.ly/1WVgt6K (Value - Motivational Video) if the link is available to watch!

4. WHERE?

Another aspect of your trajectory is the **PLACE**. There is a particular place or environment that would trigger the optimal expression of your potential. Yes, you're unique and you're created as an answer to a problem; but it would do you good to discover the specific location or community that can enhance the achievement of your purpose. From my personal experience, I am aware that each and every one of us is assigned to a particular place where we are bound to be successful. You could learn the attention and patience required by your talent. You never can tell what kind of opportunity will arise to place you in that area.

Soichiro Honda of Japan had a dream to design automobiles but never knew he would be positioned to keep providing one of the best cars in the world. Little did he know that someday he would be in the midst of those powerful and top automobile legends like Thomas Edison and Henry Ford in the hall of fame in his life time.

The right environment triggered the optimal expression of the potential of one of the greatest inventors that ever lived, Thomas Edison. At age 22 Edison was a telegraph operator when he received his first patent for a machine he called the electrographic vote-recorder. It was also recorded that Edison was one of several inventors at the time developing methods for legislative bodies, such as the US Congress, to record their votes in a more timely fashion than the time-honoured voice vote system.

Edison's vote-recorder involved a voting device connected to the clerk's desk. At the desk, the names of the legislators were embedded in metal type in two columns: "yes" and "no." Legislators would move a switch on the device to point to either "yes" or "no", sending an electric current to the device at the clerk's desk. After voting was completed, the clerk would place a chemically treated piece of paper on top of the metal type and run a metal roller over it. The current would cause the chemicals in the paper to dissolve on the side for which the vote should be recorded. "Yes" and "no" wheels kept track of the vote totals and tabulated the results.

The sky is big enough; every flying bird has their destination and path to function. Remember that the sky is your limit.

Thinking is a critical tool that can unveil innate abilities. You should look inwards and think deeply on the realm ('where') which divine providence has marked out for you to appropriately function. Please, do this and the sky will be the starting point for you in life.

Note: Check on TEDx Talk or YouTube.com to watch videos on topics relating to discovering your purpose and launching your life.

Enjoy this video http://bit.ly/2bGorNg (Caroline Myron "How to Find Your Purpose" | Super Soul Sunday | Oprah Winfrey Network) if the link is available to watch!

5. WHOM?

This aspect of your trajectory refers to **ASSOCIATION**. Yes, you are made to fulfill a purpose on earth, but no one can do that without the help and involvement of others. To achieve your goals, you need to partner with people who have a similar vision – people who can keep you on your toes just to ensure that you improve and inch closer to fulfillment. Making new good friends will give you added confidence and more structure in your life as well. You need to surround yourself with people who can challenge you and drive you forward, not those who would literally be speed-bumps on the highway!

Hang out with people who can encourage you in tough times, through the disappointments which are a part of the journey. Associate with people who can say to you *"If you can take it, you can make it."* Be strong enough to stand with those who can help you. Keep your eyes on someone who knows how to discover and nurture your gift, and always create relationships that will be rewarding.

One vital ingredient for success in life is forming and maintaining healthy relationships. Good relationships mean more fun and excitement as well as enjoying what you have in common. When you are sure that you have the support you need, you will have an easier ride through life. Your friends can offer you something new and exciting that could inspire great ideas that may improve your chances of success. As a matter of fact, associating with evil or negative people will lead you to destruction. Rather hang out with people who are well behaved. Make every effort to associate with good people whose attitude can rub off positively on you. Although you may go through good and bad times, make sure that you regard each friendship as a personal growth experience, so that you can grow as a person with a healthy mindset and obtain the support and love that you need in your life. As you take this great step, your success will come to you without stress.

"Become wise by walking with the wise; hang out with fools and watch your life fall to pieces" – Proverbs 13:20.

Note: Check on TEDx Talk or YouTube.com to watch videos on topics relating to the power of association.

Enjoy   this videohttp://bit.ly/2bQLtBq(The Power of Association - How to Fast Track Your Success) if the link is available to watch!

6. WHEN?

The **TIME** to act is today! Procrastination has proven to be the world's fastest killer of visions and dreams, as well as the most effective limitation of great goals. The time to start is not when you're older, nor when you're richer; the time to start your dream is now! The world is waiting for you – the solution! The right timing sets you on course to achieve success in any venture you put your mind to, eventually setting you on the path to better and greater things. Each day, plan and use your time wisely, and become more self-disciplined so as to achieve more. The more disciplined you are, the clearer you will be on the various aspects of your goal, making the fulfilment of your purpose much easier, and you will also experience much more peace.

In the same vein, it is also said that procrastination is a graveyard where all opportunities are buried.

Unravel your 'WHEN' by intentionally optimising your use of time via well-chosen activities, and you will soon be on the highway to a fulfilled life.

S-T-A-R-T N-O-W
Stop making excuses
   Take control of your limitations
      Act to change things now
         Reach out to get information
         Trust in your capability
            Now is the time to start
               Organise your daily routine
                  Wherever you are now is your
                     starting point

"See then that ye walk circumspectly, not as fools, but as wise. Redeeming the time, because the days are evil"– Ephesians 5:15.

Have you seen many people of retirement-age who didn't make an adequate retirement plan and are still struggling to get menial jobs? The time for you to discover your purpose and invest in hard work using the right strategies to achieve success is now. Most people today are struggling with the concern that how they are living their lives is not really in sync with their purpose. Those who fail to discover their talent – who they are created to be – will end up with hard life. Don't let that be you. Develop vision towards what you have. Work smartly and hard with the right techniques. Focus to achieve success.

Note: Check on TEDx Talk or YouTube.com to watch videos on topics relating to 'when to start your dream'.

Enjoy this video http://bit.ly/1iDRorG" if the link is available to watch!

7. VISION

As explained in my personal story, one of the most important qualities that you can cultivate is **vision**. Vision is the capacity to see beyond what your natural eyes can see, imagine the future and purpose as what relates to you. Vision is the blueprint to mastering success. Where there is no vision, goals and dreams perish. It is important to know yourself so that you can have a clearer idea of who you want to be, and the changes you need to make, whether concerning your attitudes, habits, behaviour, or perspective on life. What you see is what you will focus on, and what you focus on expands until eventually you become it. No one can discover what you have within, envision your future, or work it out for you, but only you can do that. If you do not take time to know yourself, then your vision, goals and targets for the future will be unclear.

Many people have left their future blank without vision, so they achieve nothing in future. My teacher once said that when you aim at nothing, you expect something, you get nothing.

The power to withstand difficult life situations and circumstances that threaten to put an end to one's vision is very important in pursuing one's goals. This is evident in the bible story of Joseph and Potiphar's wife. Joseph made up his mind to realise his dream vision in life. If you are familiar with the story, you will agree with me that when Joseph did not entertain the fear of rejection when he turned down the sexual advances of Potiphar's wife.

Joseph narrated his dream to his brothers, and said, I had a dream that we were all working in the field, tying stacks of wheat together. Then my stack got up. It stood there while all your stacks of wheat made a circle around mine and bowed down to it. Joseph's brothers hated and conspired against him because of his dream, and sold him to some traders, who later sold him as a slave to Potiphar. When Potiphar Joseph's master observed that the Lord was with Joseph and has made everything he was doing successful, Joseph was very diligent to his duty, Potiphar made him in charge of everything in his house except his wife. When Potiphar's wife noticed that Joseph was a good-looking guy, and because of this, she begins to entice him to sleep with her. He refused to do anything that would jeopardise the pursuit of his dream. But Joseph consistently refuses her. He says to her, my master has such trust in me; he doesn't concern himself with anything in the house except you, because you are his wife. So, how could I do such a terrible thing to my master, and sin against God. But in spite of his refusals, she persistently persuades him day after day to go to bed with her. One day, he goes into the house to do his work, and the place is empty no other servant was around. Potiphar's wife is the only one at home. She grabs him by his cloak and says "come to bed with me" but Joseph escapes out of his cloak, leaving it in her hand and runs out of the house.

When she realised that he left his cloak in her hand when he fled, she calls in her servants and says, look! *"This Hebrew tried to have sex with me, but I screamed, he left his outer garment and ran outside,"* when his master heard his wife say, *"This is the way your slave treated me,"* he became furious and took him and threw him into prison, where the king's prisoners were confined. However, Joseph's prison journey ultimately elevated him to the position of authority to rule over all the land of Egypt, where his brothers came to bow down to him to buy grain as he had envisioned early in life.

What is vision?

Vision is the ability to see, the capability to think about, or plan the future with imagination with a vivid picture in view to deciding what you want. It is the main **MAP** to your success. MAP represents: **Mindset-Action-Process**

M = Mindset. This is the belief a person holds about his/her qualities and abilities. Some believe they can develop their talent and abilities while others feel they can't develop their abilities and talent to turning your vision into reality

A = Action. Practical step to achieve your ideas

P = Process. Procedures to follow in idea realisation

Having a vision of who you are, and clear vision of what you want to become in life is the vital thing to consider to achieving a better future. Vision prepares you for the journey you are about to take, gives you something specific to strive toward, and helps you to attract success with the power of your mind, moving from imagination to reality. Vision is what it takes to face your fears and become a champion. The fact that you are not where you want to be now does not mean that you will never make it.

No matter what happens to you or around you, stay motivated and stay focused on what you desire. Be prepared to overcome any difficulties.

Your vision is the staircase that helps you to work diligently, passionately, and against all odds to succeed and excel. Vision is the fertilizer that gives you the wisdom and knowledge to find your breakthrough opportunity. Vision is what encourages you to take responsibility for your achievements. Good things usually happen when there is vision. If you are a human being and you have no vision, then your life is not going anywhere.

Vision is comprised of 4 main parts

- **Motive**: this is the purpose of your idea, what you intent to achieve. You should have a clear understanding of what your idea is all about.

- **Mission statement**: this is a statement which is used to specify the feature of your idea, and the strategic actions plan you will take to accomplish your ideas.

- **Vivid narrative**: description of the process to articulate your vision with vivid picture, showing why your idea exists, what it represents, what exactly you do, and how this procedure can help you actualise your dream.

- **Value**: Ensuring the integrity of your products and services are of great worth. Illustrate in details the uniqueness of your products and services; highlight all the good factors you offer that your competitors don't have.

Now that you have come to know yourself and identified your beliefs, values, and principles, it's important to decide what you want to focus on, using pictures. Describe as fully as you can your vision of your career path, including the knowledge, skills, and attitudes you have now and how best to improve yourself. These will give you the competence to help you achieve your vision. For example, personally, I knew that I was a bit impatient with people; even my family and friends complained about it. I recognised that this was something I wanted to change about my attitudes. After college, I realised that I needed to gain professional knowledge and skills so that I could become a counselling psychologist helping young people to understand themselves so as to create their vision for the future and avoid the pain I went through during my early teenage years without goals and vision.

The vision process

In order to attain my goal, I identified some milestones in my life vision and the time to get on the go. Where to start is to know the details, I developed a vision map of what I wanted to be to measure my success. I made sure that the vision I set out for my future was specific, measurable, attainable (not too big) and realistic. Finally, I added a timeline for achieving my vision. My vision was: completing a

National Certificate in Education and obtaining a bachelor's degree in Education Guidance and Counselling by the age of 25; completing a Master's degree in Education Counselling Psychology by the age of 28; earning a PhD by the age 36 and working with schools and different organisations involving young people worldwide by the age 38.

However, as you know, life has its own twists and turns and unanticipated detours. I hit a pothole regarding my goal of attaining my PhD. After my Master's degree, I got married and started a business running multinational companies. My husband became a top political figure, but my passion to help young people overcome the plight of youth violence became my top desire. In 2007, I decided to leave everything to go back to school for a PhD degree in the United Kingdom to improve my knowledge in order to make a difference in the lives of the young people.

Hitting potholes

The process of studying towards my PhD has been a long, rough road. I have gained a Graduate Diploma in Psychology and now hold another Master of Philosophy degree in Psychology in the United Kingdom. I am still marching towards the finish-line for my PhD. Even though I didn't anticipate these problems, I adjusted my goals accordingly because I'm seeing the uncertain future of many young people today and hope that, by knowing who they are, they can become the great leaders of tomorrow. During this process, I have published 5 books and developed a programme for helping young people to discover their potential and implement their ideas, producing products and services and marketing them to create their own business. Of my books "*The Successful Student*" reveals factors that help students to develop good attitudes towards their studies. Such attitudes are hardly ever taught in school, yet they inhibit students from achieving a higher academic performance. This book was featured on the *SecEed.co.uk* website for a month and in different media publications in the United Kingdom. Today, it has been published in more than 9 countries.

In life it doesn't matter where you start. The most important thing you need to do is to believe in yourself. You need to imagine what you can become, and accept responsibility for functioning in the capacity in which you find yourself. Taking the initiative will help you to manifest your ideas and get them out into the world, helping the people you are meant to help. When you develop your sense of self-worth, you become a vehicle through which all else around you is affected and sustained. You create your source of income and establish a financial future.

You may not have anyone who can instill a sense of purpose in your life, but you can overcome your fears and develop the self-confidence to learn from life and from others around you who made it from nothing. In my own case, no one put the spring into my heels to act to create the kind of life I should have. I realised that myself, and started to chart the course of my future which I am living by today. Remember, what you focus on will expand; you become what your mind think. By taking action on matters, you discover the treasures that will lead you to success. When your confidence is greater, your aim is sharper, your mindset is more positive, and what you envision is more likely to materialise into a reality. Believe in your ability to focus on the bright side of life. Become more conscious of your innate abilities, thought patterns, and your state of mind in order to determine your destiny.

Note: Check on TEDx Talk or YouTube.com for videos on topics relating to vision.Watch "Philosophy for a Happy Life":

Enjoy this video http://bit.ly/1iLfdgE (My philosophy for a happy life | Sam Berns | TEDxMidAtlantic) if the link is available to watch!

Your vision exercise

The main purpose of this exercise is to encourage you to think freely, creatively and imaginatively about your direction and potential.

Imagine you have been given a fortune to fix everything you want in your life. Now the question is: Given such free choice,

- What would you want to do?

- What skills would you love to develop?

- Can you picture exactly what you want to do?

The important thing is that you can visualise and consider what you would do if you had a free choice. So what's actually stopping you from pursuing your dream? Think it through carefully. In most cases, the obstacles will be self-imposed. Although it might not always be easy to do things you want to do, most things are possible. You don't necessarily need to have four or five years of formal education to become who you want to be and follow a new direction. It starts with understanding that your future is in your own hands. You and not anyone or anything else determines whether you follow your own passions and achieve your own potential, or regret never trying at all.

Your visualisation and beliefs:

Visualisation is seeing with your inner mental eyes, the consciousness of creating your desired outcome in life. The important key to everything you create is your vision of the future. Here visualise your various goals and ideas, to bring the future into the present, as if it has already happened. At the same time, you are processing out your deep-rooted limiting beliefs that always precede reality since they were acquired early in your life and has been incorporated into your consciousness. These are the negative obstacles on the pathway to achieving your idea.

Write down all your visualisation below with great clarity and vividness in order to be effective.

_____

_____

_____

Note: Check on TEDx Talk or YouTube.com to watch videos on topics relating to the power of vision.

Enjoy   this video:http://bit.ly/2ceuv3W(the Power of Vision part1   Dr Myles Munroe) if the link is available to watch!

Your decision to make most of your potential today

What is your take when it comes to making most of your potential? Ask yourself these three questions.

- What have I decided on how to make most of your potential?

- If so, when should I make that decision?

- What exactly will I do?

Your Discipline Every Day

Based on the decision you have made of making most of your potential, what is the discipline you will practice daily to make most of your potential?

Transformation Action

Action is the key that will help you develop your ideas

- watch video studies on YouTube relating to your decision to help you grow

- discuss with those that can help you

- read short inspiration to help you start a habit to work with your idea

Look out for great opportunities to grow

Chapter 13

Ideas from young minds that have changed the world

"With a generation of younger folks who have thrived on the success of their companies, there is a big opportunity for many of us to give back earlier in our lifetime and see the impact of our philanthropic efforts." — Mark Zuckerberg.

As a kid you likely wanted to be an astronaut or doctor or a famous football player. If you are like most people, you had big dreams, desires and aspirations for your life.

However, life got in the way and those dreams and ambitions you once had then faded with it. Think about what happened to this life that you always imagined.

Looking back now, would you be able to describe your vision in detail? If you can't, you are not alone. If you can, do you know how to create enough income and time to make that idea a reality?

Ideas beautify the world in which we live. Our dreams are their main motivating force. In this age, when many young people today are unsure of their life's purpose, many others are changing the course of history by coming up with creative ideas and innovations. Some young people have shown that they are not just the future we hope for, but that they are also the present. They have demonstrated their ability to change the world with their wits, wisdom, feelings and ideas. Several young people have used their ideas for repairing a world divided by uncertainty, hatred, fear and violence.

With the right mindset, strategy, resources, connections, and opportunities, any young person can make a mark on the world with a great idea. In this chapter we will take a look at the stories of some young people whose ideas has made great impact in the world today.

Young people who have realised their great ideas.

Alexander Graham Bell

Bell was a researcher from Scotland who had a strong interest in the world. This led to his experimenting with technological designs at a young age, such as a simple dehusking device when he was aged 12.

Due to his mother being deaf, he was motivated to study acoustics. In 1874 the essential idea of the telephone formed in his mind. This ultimately resulted in the innovation of the telephone. Bell's telephone grew out of enhancements he made to the telegraph. He had actually designed the "harmonic telegraph" which might send out more than one message at a time over a single telegraph wire. His path to success was not as clear as one may suppose; it was rather surrounded by many previous failures.

Mark Zuckerberg

Zuckerberg developed an interest in computers at an early age. When he was about 12, he used *Atari BASIC* to create a messaging programme which he named *"Zucknet"*. At age 10, Mark was bored with school. Noticing this, his father introduced him to his *Altair* computer. Together they wrote a programme that connected the computer at home with the computer in the office. They called it "ZuckNet". It alerted Doctor Z, as Mark Zuckerberg's father is known, when a patient arrived. It worked better than having the receptionist yell, "Patient here!"

Mark quickly learned everything his father knew about computers. He started studying with a tutor. Then he started taking a college class in computer science while still in middle school. He read books. But he really started learning to code when he transferred to a private school where he met a programming whiz kid Adam D'Angelo. Together they started hacking. They made an artificially intelligent music player that learned the user's musical tastes. Soon Microsoft found out about it and offered money and a job. Zuckerberg was not interested.

This is an ongoing theme about how Mark Zuckerberg operated. He was offered millions, even billions, at least 11 times, and every time he walked away. Each time, he had a new idea, a bigger plan.

The creator of the social network *Facebook*, Mark Zuckerberg is one of the youngest billionaires on the planet, and *Facebook* now has more than 1 billion active users.

Adam Horwitz

Horwitz was a UK online financier who had a passion for his mobile phone business. Building up a monopoly at a young age, he earned a six-figure profit by selling apps. From this, he invented an advertising service for business called the *Yeptext idea*. He makes great amount of money online, and his best advice for those who chase the same dream is *"Just do it."*

Pablo Ruiz Picasso

Picasso was a Spanish artist who had a special skill in painting, which was apparent from a young age. Integrating various methods, theories and concepts, he is among the most prominent figures in 20th century art. Picasso's enthusiasm for art was soon revealed to the world. Picasso demonstrated extraordinary artistic talent in his early years, painting in a naturalistic manner through his childhood and adolescence. During the first decade of the 20th century, his style changed as he experimented with different theories, techniques, and ideas. Conquering many obstacles, he accomplished great success and fortune in his lifetime. Picasso stated: "*Action is the fundamental secret to all success.*" Resolving to act rather than remaining idle will certainly produce energy for success.

Anthony Halmon

Halmon was a young father who created a pacifier with an inbuilt thermometer. A native Chicagoan, Halmon described Chicago's Englewood area as a "*tough, rough*" place with "*a lot of violence and gangs.*" Growing up, he said, he was accosted regularly by various gang members due to the reputation of one of his relatives. The year that his father died (his sophomore year in high school) was also the year in which he learned he was to be a father. The teen made it his goal to better his life for the sake of his daughter, who is now 3 years old.

Interested in studying sociology and government, Halmon was the only a freshman at Cornell University, but he'd already made a name for himself. In 2013, the young father came up with the idea of creating a pacifier that doubles as a thermometer, called the *Thermofier*. His creation is described as an improvement on existing models. The idea came from his concern for his young daughter; he worried that he could not easily discern when the baby wasn't feeling well. His invention earned him a visit to the White House and a meeting with President Obama.

Andrew Pelham

Pelham was an 11-year old who invented a gadget that could potentially save lives. After learning that approximately 38 children in America die each year from being left in hot cars, young Andrew Pelham felt compelled to do something. He entered *The Rubber Band Contest for Young Inventors*, which is held each year in Akron, Ohio – the city is also known as the rubber capital of the United States. There is only one rule for contestants: they must use rubber bands in their invention. With that in mind, Andrew created the *E-Z Baby Saver*, a cheap way to help parents remember when they have a child in the back seat. A simple device made of duct tape and rubber bands, it is a strap that stretches from the back seat to the front and attaches to the driver's door, rendering the driver unable to walk away from the car when a child is still inside. The invention won second place and US$500.Andrew used his prize money to buy a laptop and create his website.

Tyler Dikman

Dikman began his career as a technology guru aged ten, when he began to accumulate money like water. He started his career with magic shows at birthday parties and used to charge around $25 for his one-minute performance. He got his first computer when he was ten and, at that early age, became so interested in the computer system that he taught himself to be proficient in it. In fact, he developed a high level of skills, a plan, and learned to examine an application and the intricacies of distributed design. He used to repair computers for his teachers and charged them $15 per hour. Later he got a job at Merrill Lynch by babysitting the children of the vice president of Merrill Lynch, Malcolm Taaffe. At age 15, he started his own company, *Cooltronics* and made his career in this technology line. He is the youngest technology entrepreneur and was a millionaire by age 25.

Kylie Simonds

Simonds is the 11-year old cancer survivor who invented a chemotherapy bag. When she was 8 years old, Kylie Simonds of Naugatuck, Connecticut, was diagnosed with rhabdomyosarcoma, a cancer of the connective tissues. She is now in remission and recovering from the ordeal. Throughout her illness, one of the obstacles she endured was IV pole wires that would cause her constantly to trip. She also needed help pushing the pole around because it was too heavy for her. Kylie invented a *paediatric IV backpack* – a wearable, portable IV machine for children receiving chemotherapy or transfusions. The bag even comes in colourful designs. She calls it the *I-Pack*. Kylie's design won a prize at the Connecticut Invention Convention in August 2014. She has secured a patent and is trying to raise money to put the backpack into production.

Mallory Kievman

Kievman is the13-year old who invented a lollipop that cures hiccups after she was afflicted with a stubborn case of the hiccups two years before. She decided to test a number of folk remedies, from sipping water out of an upside-down cup to drinking salt water. Eventually, after curing her hiccups, the future doctor combined her three favourite remedies to form her own cure for the annoying ailment: sugar, apple cider vinegar, and lollipops. While she claims she is still in the process of *"tweaking the taste"*, her invention has already received a considerable amount of attention and a patent is pending. In 2012, she launched a potentially lucrative business built around her unusual cure for hiccups.She has enlisted MBA students to assist in launching her start-up.

Kenneth Shinozuka

Shinozuka is the grandson of an Alzheimer patient who created a sensor for patients with dementia. The New York teenager, aged 15, won a $50,000 science prize for developing wearable sensors that send mobile alerts when a dementia patient begins to wander away from their bed. He said his invention was inspired by his grandfather's symptoms, which frequently caused him to wander from bed in the middle of the night and hurt himself. His invention uses coin-sized wireless sensors that are worn on the feet of a potential wanderer. The sensors detect pressure caused when the person stands up, triggering an audible alert on a caregiver's smartphone using an app. The award that he won honours a project that aims to make a practical difference by addressing an environmental, health or resources challenge.

Jack Andraka

Andraka was the 15-year-oldsophomore prodigy who created a pancreatic cancer detection tool. Over 85 percent of all pancreatic cancers are diagnosed late, when someone has a less-than-two-percent chance of survival. So when news broke in 2011 that a test had been developed that might detect early pancreatic cancer, the research world not only took notice, it went into shock – for the test hadn't been developed by some renowned cancer research institute, but by a 15-year-old high school freshman named Jack Andraka. Jack convinced an eminent cancer researcher to let him use his laboratory to develop his theory, all before he even had his driver's license. While the test must undergo years of clinical trials, the biotech industry has already beaten a path to Jack's door. Jack beat 1,500 contestants to win the grand prize at the Intel International Science Fair with his invention. The self-described science geek received $100,000 in prize money.

Louis Braille

Braille was born in 1809 in Coupvray, France. As a young man, Braille found a way to make the world a better place by conquering the unpleasant circumstances that life had hurled at him. At the age of 3, an eye injury left him blind. Studying at the *Royal Institute for Blind Youth in Paris*, Louis invented a system of reading and writing for the blind involving raised dots, which today is known as Braille. At age 19, Braille became a full-time teacher at the *Royal Institute*, where he remained until his death at age 43.

Today, Braille is a universally used tactile method of writing and reading for the blind. Several studies have shown that congenitally blind adults who learned to read using Braille have higher employment rates and educational levels, were more financially self-sufficient, and spent more time reading than did those who learned to read using print.

Frank Epperson

Epperson was a typical American who, at age 11, invented a *"frozen beverage on a stick,"* now called the "**Popsicle**," that would later end up being an <u>ingenious concept</u>. After blending powdered soda with water to make soda water, he inadvertently left the blending container outside on an uncommonly cold night. The mixture froze solid, with the wooden stirring stick standing upright. It gave him the idea of creating a frozen beverage for consumption. There was one big issue: he needed an industrial freezer for his Popsicle assembly line. Starting in 1923, Epperson applied for a series of patents to secure the design for his *"frozen confectionery."* He pressed through rejection and failure without giving up until he had accomplished a strong concept, which included marking his name on the sticks. The patent documents discuss consistency (*"syrup results in a crystalline product of hard snowy consistency"*), stick material (*"employ a wooden stick of relatively porous though sapless and tasteless wood"*), freezing method (*"rapid refrigeration results in a more uniform product"*), and vessel shape (*"ordinary test tubes"*). The **Popsicle** was officially born.

Bill Gates

Gates is the co-founder of American multinational technology company *Microsoft Corporation*, and is one of the best-known entrepreneurs in the field of the personal computer. Some see him as an innovative visionary who sparked a computer revolution. Others criticise his business tactics for being predatory and stifling competition in the software industry. Regardless of what his supporters and detractors may think, Bill Gates is possibly the *most successful entrepreneur* of the 20th century. In just 25 years, he developed a two-man operation into a multibillion-dollar colossus, making himself the richest man in the world. He accomplished this feat, not by inventing new technology, but by taking existing technology and adapting it to a specific market. Eventually he dominated that market through innovative promotion and cunning business savvy.

Gates's first exposure to computers came while he was attending the prestigious Lakeside School in Seattle. A local company offered the school the use of its computer through a Teletype link, and young Gates became entranced by the possibilities of the primitive machine. Along with fellow student Paul Allen, he began ditching class to work in the school's computer room. Their work would soon pay off. At 15, Gate conceived the idea of starting a business, and he and Allen went into business together. The two teens netted $20,000 with *Traf-O-Data*, a programme they developed to measure traffic flow in the Seattle area.

Nick D'Aloisio

At age 18, D'Aloisio was one of the young people utilising his potential to make a significant impact on our world today. He was declared *"the teenager who has changed the way the world reads."* D'Aloisio designed an app called *Summly*, which sums up news articles in just a few sentences. Investors saw great value and potential in this London teen's app, and Yahoo recently bought the app from D'Aloisio for $30 million. Other investors in D'Aloisio's work includes Ashton Kutcher, Yoko Ono, and Wendi Murdoch.

The teen has been designing apps since he was 12 years old – on a Mac under his father's licensing information – with little to no tech background. Self-driven, he began to learn about programming and studied extensively. The hard work has certainly paid off for him!

Steve Jobs

Jobs's life history was not a straight line, but more like a winding path. It is clear that Jobs had no grand plan early on in his life. His search for himself took him through India, Buddhism, psychedelic drug use, and attempts to become an astronaut and start a computer company in the Soviet Union. He found inspiration and creativity in himself at certain periods of his life. If there is a pattern of creativity and genius, his life's timeline can reveal it.

In 2005, at a Stanford talk titled "How to Live Before You Die,"Steve Jobs summarised his guiding principle in life. He said that you've got to find what you love. And that is as true for your work as it is for your lovers. Your work is going to fill a large part of your life, and the only way to be truly satisfied is to do what you believe is great work. And the only way to do great work is to love what you do. If you haven't found it yet, keep looking. Don't settle. As with all matters of the heart, you'll know when you find it. And, like any great relationship, it just gets better and better as the years roll on.

Steve's advice to any young person wanting to discover an idea is to keep looking. Don't settle. "*Sometimes life hits you in the head with a brick. Don't lose faith.*"

You have the potential to create your own super brand and to entice people with your imaginative ideas, thereby launching you into the wider world. You are creative and have an eye for detail. You have the knowledge and wisdom to do the impossible. You do not have to be a genius, but you do have to have a keen sense of self-worth and confidence to find your purpose, accomplish your goals and achieve financial freedom.

Note: Check on TEDx Talk or YouTube.com to watch videos on topics relating to the art of creativity, innovation and idea creation.

Enjoy this video http://bit.ly/1LILYsE (The Art of Creativity | Taika Waititi | TEDxDoha) and http://bit.ly/1rIqOEA (Creative thinking - how to get out of the box and generate ideas: Giovanni Corazza at TEDxRoma) if the links are available to watch!

Your decision on ideas from young minds that changed the world today

What is your take when it comes to ideas from young minds that have changed the world? Ask yourself these three questions.

- What have I decided on ideas that have changed the world?

- If so, when should I make that decision?

- What exactly will I do?

Your Discipline Every Day

Based on the decision you have made on ideas from young minds that have changed the world, what is the discipline you will practice daily to have an idea that can change the world?

Transformation Action

Action is the key that will help you develop your ideas

- watch video studies on YouTube relating to your decision to help you grow

- discuss with those that can help you

- read short inspiration to help you start a habit to work with your idea

Look out for great opportunities to grow

Section 3: Action Strategies

This section comprises of activities that will take 15 minutes to an hour to complete, with clear and concise step-by-step procedures for you to follow. Here, you will find simple to use and easy to understand exercises that can help you to achieve your goals and dream idea to generate income.

Chapter 14

Action

"Action is the foundational key to all success" – Pablo Picasso.

The dog blanket

I like to start with a short story about and the dog blanket. Rachel told a story of how she got a vision of an idea to develop blanket for dogs.

She wrote down the vision and how she intended to carry out the project but did nothing about it again.

She narrated how she went for an exhibition with a friend two years after and found that the award winner was a lady with exact vision she had.

She said at the end of the conference, she had a chat with the lady and discovered that it was the same time she had that vision and didn't take action on it.

I explain the concept of Action as the act of doing something to bring about desired result. Nothing will happen to your life situation until you do something about it. Your ideas come true when something is done to accomplish the vision for your ideas.

In pursuit to achieving your idea, it is important to note that Success is the CAR which moves on the wheel called **action**.

Action is the bedrock of making any vision a reality. Those who have big vision and do nothing end in frustration.

When you have great vision for your idea, you must have strategic action drive to achieve it otherwise your vision will lead to great disappointment.

Action is the most important process you can employ to actualise your idea. When you feel afraid that your set goals cannot be reached and your plans and ideas cannot be attained, do not adjust the goals; rather adjust the action procedure *by* simply stepping into the wheel named Action!

The authenticity is that you have the ideas within you to change your life, in terms of stabilising your relationships, improving your finances, attaining greater career success, improving your business, and deciding what you want to be a success.

Your action towards your goals, time management and milestone today determine where you will be in the future.

How To Effectively Maintain Your Action Plan

I came up with acronym for **ACTION**:

A –*Assign* a time to everything daily — time to work, eat, exercise and rest

C - *Consciously* prepare, arrange on how carry out your action plan

T - *Take* control of your life and your future today

I - ***Invest*** mentally in your visions and goals daily

O - ***Organise*** every aspect of what you do daily

N - ***No*** excuses should be tolerated

Managing stress

To effectively take action on your vision, Stress management is a great step to master to avoid distraction.

- Learn breathing and relaxation techniques and practice them on a daily basis.

- Take a regular break, such as walking away from your desk for 10 minutes or getting some fresh air for 10 minutes.

- Get better organised by making a daily list of tasks that you know you can achieve; be realistic.

- Make another list of tasks that may be more challenging to achieve and work out how you could achieve them.

- Sort out your worries. Make a list of things that are worrying you and try and tackle them one by one.

- Change what you can, and do your best to accept what you can't change.

- Learn to say no. You can't please everyone, and remember to look after yourself.

- Improve your overall lifestyle by eating regular, nutritionally balanced meals and exercising daily.

- Adopt a healthy work-life balance.

- Keep a positive diary and list five positive things about your day; it can be as little as being aware of the sun shining. No negative things can go in your diary!

The point to note about developing your idea is that, that same idea is given to different people in the universe at the same time, but only those who take action succeed with it.

Success is woven in the very fiber of action and discipline.

Chapter 15:

How to turn your life around

The process of making changes in your life is largely determined by who you are. It is your attitude towards your set objectives that defines your achievement to maximise your talent to develop ideas. The potency of your habits determines the greatness of your goal attainment; and your mindset is vital in determining how your life turns around. By believing in the vision for your ideas, and taking necessary action steps, you can take a decision today on how to accomplish your most important dream idea.

Turnaround steps:

Self-diagnosis

- What do you value most?

| |
| |
| |

- What unique talent do you have that can help or benefit people in any given situation?

| |
| |
| |

- What type of work do you love to do most?

- What type of work do you dislike to do?

- What thought do you think most often when you reflect on yourself and your environment?

Take a moment to contemplate these questions. Complete them all as honestly as you can.

Your sincere answers to these questions are already aligned with what you have within you.

Identifying barriers

Barriers could be described as an obstacle that prevents you from moving forward or having access to proceed to your destination.

Barriers can affect you throughout your life and delay you in achieving your confidence and your dreams. Barriers may be related to your capabilities, clarity, possibilities or the tasks involved. The following statements can help to highlight those areas that may be delaying you from making a start and moving forward. They will help you ascertain what you need to address in order to achieve your dream.

Action exercise

- Choose a dream that you'd like to achieve and write it down in this box so it is clear in your mind.

- State your dream in terms of five statements and write each statement in the line below. For example, creating a new marketing idea, exploring a new intellectual idea, testing a new business approach, planning and setting the goals.

1 _____

2 _____

3 _____

4 _____

5 _____

Say each statement aloud. You will remember the statement better. But if you cannot do this, then go through them mentally several times to remind yourself.

- For each statement, rate your degree of conviction in your dream, with 1 being the lowest and 5 the highest degree of belief. The lowest scores will highlight areas you need to work on initially, whilst the higher scores show you areas in which you feel more positive about yourself.

- Be aware of how you feel and what thoughts go through your mind as you score each statement. These thoughts may provide some useful messages during the exercise.

- Ask yourself what else you need to help address the areas highlighted. For example, if you score a low number for statement 4 in relation to "capabilities," you will need to consider what specifically you need to do to develop the capabilities to achieve your dream.

Once you have assessed your degree of confidence in these areas of belief, consider whether there are other resources that you might need. If so, write down these 5 resources.

1_____

2_____

3_____

4_____

5_____

Do you need other people to help you in any way? If yes, write down 5 people you may need their help.

1_____

2_____

3_____

4_____

5_____

Dreams

Rate the following statements concerning your dream, with 1 meaning *"disagree strongly"* and 5 meaning *"agree strongly."*

1. My dream is desirable and worthwhile

1 2 3 4 5

2. It is possible to achieve my dream

1 2 3 4 5

3. What I have to do to achieve my dream is clear   1 2 3 4 5

4. The envisaged outcome of my dream is appropriate   1 2 3 4 5

5. The envisaged outcome of my dream fits in with my lifestyle   1 2 3 4 5

6. I have the capabilities necessary to achieve my dream   1 2 3 4 5

7. I deserve to achieve my dream

1 2 3 4 5

Action exercise

Write down 5 top things holding you back.

1_____

2_____

3_____

4_____

5_____

Consider your daily priorities

- What area of your life do you want to improve?

- Which aspects of your life would you like to understand better?

- Why do you react in certain ways to different situations?

- Which habits or patterns of behaviour do you often repeat?

- Could you improve how you react to yourself and certain situations?

Setting your outcome

Setting your outcome involves taking time to consider your dreams or what you want to achieve. When developing your ideas, it is important to use a simple smart procedure to help you manage your performance and setting the way your ideas turns out in the end. Your ideas should be:

S-M-A-R-T

- **S** - *Simple and positive*: Dreams that are achievable within a given timeframe.

- **M** – *Meaningful and suitable*: Something tangible to bring the desired result.

- **A** – *Accountable*: See yourself as fully committed to achieving your dream.

- **R** – *Ready and right*: Ensure that you are ready to take the necessary step without a doubt, something exactly good for you now.

- **T – *Transform***: Ensure it's the right step to take to bring transformational change in your life.

How To Maximise The Best Within

The Truth About Yourself

There is no limitation to what you can do. Your limiting beliefs are the only barrier that can hold you back from realising all the possibilities before you. You have more potential within you than you think. You have more creative power than you can ever imagine. Believe in possibility. Pay attention to the fears you're experiencing in your life now. When you mentally concentrate upon the condition which you desire to see manifest in your life, you can awaken great ideas to create your business.

Take Hold Of Your Dream Ideas

- You have great potential within.
- Be proactive and positive
- Understand how to use positive experiences to develop a resource bank.
- Deal with the negative situations in order to stop repeating old habits.
- Considering an issue from all perspectives often helps to avoid a challenging situation.
- When you are consciously aware of your ideas, you can decide if you believe they are true or not, and how they may help you with a particular situation.

- Practicing changing your mindset maps, not the reality before you now.

Functions Of Your Mind

If you can put your mind to think enough, your future is full of great prospect. Resourceful states of mind generate great ideas, which set the pace for successful outcome of your ideas. Having the image of the ideas you want fully printed in your mind is a vital key to its accomplishment.

- Realise that you have within yourself all the resources you need to achieve what you want.
- The emphasis is on your internal thoughts (internal dialogue) and creating a resourceful state of mind.

Beliefs, Memories And Values

- Your beliefs, memories, values and experiences affect how you perceive and interpret life events and business challenges.

- Beliefs help you to make sense of the world around you and can either empower you to achieve success or limit your thinking about your progress.

Memories

- Memories can affect your present and future.

- Unless you are conscious of them, your memories can lead

unconsciously to a negative response.

Values

- Values drive your behaviour and can either motivate or reduce your enthusiasm.

- Values also affect your choice of friends, hobbies, interests and how you spend your time.

Why Beliefs Are Important

- Your experiences are coded, ordered, stored and replayed through language and other forms of communication (pictures, sounds, feelings, tastes, smells).

- You will remember what you want of a certain situation.

Changing Negative Beliefs To Achieve Success

- You can adjust the sub-modalities (that is, the intensity of a feeling or a sound) to diminish the sensation so that you can adjust how you think about it.

- You can then increase the positive beliefs or values you would like to try out.

- There is no failure, only feedback

- The brain works by trial and error.

- Mistakes can become opportunities for learning and growth.

Enabling and Limiting Beliefs

- Our beliefs can be positive and enabling, or limiting and negative.

- Consider which of the next following examples you identify with to determine whether you are more inclined to use limiting or enabling beliefs.

Enabling Beliefs

- *'I can do that'*

- *'I'm good at...'*

- *'I achieve my goals'*

- *'I'm learning a new skill'*

- *'Being different is good'*

- *'I can see the glass is half full with space for more'*

- *'Let me have a go'*

Limiting Beliefs

- *'Failing an exam is painful'*

- *'I can't sing'*

- *'I'm useless at...'*

- *'I was never any good at...'*

- *'I always do it wrong'*

- *'I can't do ... as well as ...'*

- *'I'm too ... short/ thin/ fat/ tall'*

- *'It is too difficult'*

- *'They won't like me'*

Creating A Positive Belief

- In your mind's eye, imagine the worrying event occurring in the future.

- Now imagine floating out in time to 15 minutes after the successful completion of the event.

- Next, think again about the event itself and notice how you feel about the success, now in the present time.

- Remaining in the present moment, consider how your level of concern or anxiety has altered.

Your Brain

- Understanding how you create thoughts and how brain pathways develop can provide insights into how you deal with certain situations, consciously and unconsciously.

- Learning how to change habits and rewire your thinking can be a valuable tool.

Neurons And Brain Pathways

- Brain cells or neurons are responsible for your thinking.

- As you think, imagine or learn something, messages are passed between brain cells forming a neural pathway.

- Each neuron communicates by releasing chemicals called

neurotransmitters, which carry messages between the neurons.

- Dendrites and axons connect each neuron.

- Relaxation and sleep are essential for memorising and learning.

- Following the right diet is vital for memory and reasoning.

Formation Of Habits

- When you learn new skills, a new pattern is established in the brain.

- Each time you repeat the skills, the pattern becomes clearer.

- The more you practice a new skill, the more the connections grow in the brain.

How To Think

These examples highlight where re-wiring of your thinking may be helpful:

- Gaining a new perspective

- Trying something new

- Replacing negative thoughts with positive ones

- Exchanging limiting thoughts with enabling thoughts

- Encouraging new ideas and creativity

- Altering old habits

- Developing new approaches to situations

Rewiring Your Thinking

- *'I can't, it won't work'*

  The negative pathway is developed

- *'I can't, it won't work'*
  The negative pathway becomes a habit

- *'I can, it may work'*

  A new pathway is created

- *'I can, it will work'*

  The new positive habit is created

- To *rewire* your thinking, you need to *be willing to take risks* and occasionally *do things differently*.

- It is estimated that it takes *21 days to create a new habit* and to allow the new brain pathways to develop, challenge yourself to give it a chance to transform things around.

Thoughts Can Affect Your Idea Creation

- Watch what you repeatedly think of, your thoughts become words

- Watch what you say often, your words become actions

- Watch what you spend time doing, your actions become habits

- Watch what you repeatedly do, your habits become character

- Watch how you react always, your character becomes your destiny

(Adapted from an anonymous Chinese proverb)

Your Decision To Turn Your Life Around Today

What is your take when it comes to how to turn your life around? Ask yourself these three questions.

- What have I decided on how to turn my life around?

- If so, when should I make that decision?

- What exactly will I do?

Your Discipline Every Day

Based on the decision you have made to turn your life around, what is the discipline you will practice daily to turn your life around?

Transformation Action

Action is the key that will help you develop your ideas

- watch video studies on YouTube relating to your decision to help you grow

- discuss with those that can help you

- read short inspiration to help you start a habit to work with your idea

Look out for great opportunities to grow

Chapter 16

Goal-setting

Definition

The term *goal-setting* refers to planning and writing down what you need to do to arrive at a pre-determined destination. If you are going to travel from the United Kingdom to Germany, then reaching Germany would be your final goal and you would need a strategy to get there – that is, a step-by-step process to reach your desired destination. Example for your trip to Germany, you need to book a ticket with an airline, making travel plans from your home to the airport and to your final destination in Germany.

Principles for Goal-Setting

- Make a list of everything you want to do

- Start with goals that can be achieved within a year

- Select a single project to work towards this goal and focus on achieving this goal before starting on any others

- Set yourself daily reminders about achieving your goal

- Set a time of completion of each project

- Immerse yourself in your project so as to feel your goal.

Action exercise: Goal-Setting activity

The purpose of this exercise is for you to develop a plan of action for reaching your desired goals.

Complete the following table to make a start now on your goals.

Goals	Evidence	Outcome or operation
Present state or problem – where are you	How do you know you've met	Actions to achieve the outcome

at?	your goals	and a back-up plan. What process will you need to put in place?
Desired state or outcome – where do you want to go?	What will it look like?	
	What will it feel like?	
	What will people say?	

	How will others know?	
	Is it win-win?	
Your goals:	**Your evidence:**	**Your actions:**

Model for Achieving Your Idea

When developing your ideas, it is important to follow simple and easy to use guideline to help you achieve your goals faster.

Here, I have put together a unique eight point practical model to facilitate your active involvement to accomplishing the goals for those great ideas systematically.

This easy-to-use model will help you to create a personal roadmap as you write down your short-term, intermediate-term, and long-term goals to leverage every opportunity to monetize your own idea.

- Short-term goals are those goals that you can achieve in less than three months

- Intermediate-term goals are those goals you can achieve within three to six months, although some may take up to 12 months to completion.

- Long-term goals are those goals that take more than one year or more to accomplish.

Cognitive psychologist affirms that the act of writing down what you want accesses a different part of your brain and makes a deal between your hand, mind, and your heart. It has been proven that by writing down long-term perspectives, you are more likely to achieve them.

Model Step One: *Make it simple*

- Write out your dream idea, make it as simple as possible and design the process so it is realistically achievable.

_____

_____

Model Step Two: *Make it clear*

- Be very clear about your passion and motivation, on the main reason you want to achieve that idea. Assign dates by when you will achieve each step of the idea, and describe them in as much detail as you can.

_____

_____

Model Step Three: *Strategies to support*

- Write out major strategies you have learnt from experts that will support you accomplish goals for your great idea

_____

_____

Model Step Four: *An end Picture*

- Have an *"end picture"* in mind or draw a picture that depicts your idea as if it has already happened

_____

_____

Model Step Five: *Handle obstacles*

- Write how you intend to handle any obstacle that may come your way during this process. Write down your focus areas

_____

_____

Model Step Six: *Make a plan*

- Map out a visible representation of your activities, keep record of everything, layout schedule and put timeline on everything. Plan how to break large tasks into smaller, manageable size, and how you wish to celebrate your success.

_____

_____

Model Step Seven: *Action steps*

- Make adequate action steps you will follow, milestones, monthly schedule, daily schedule, allocating the day and time to accomplish each step on your path to success. How you plan to source your materials, steps to follow-up on your schedules, people to contact and persons involved.

Write out a time frame for each task in presence tense, with a date, like this:

-Today is (date), and I....... (time)

-Today is (date), I will .... (time .... 15 minutes, 1 hour, etc)

Do something every day that moves you towards achieving your ideas (your list of action plan each day will help ground your frame of mind positively).Give your task a deadline when to accomplish each step.

Make daily list of tasks you earnestly need to complete before going to bed, studies show that what you focus on before going to sleep is ingrain in your subconscious mind. Place your written goal where you can see them daily, maybe by your bedside or keep them in your drawer, by your mirror. My roommate in the university keeps hers next to her pillow so in the morning when she wakes up she reviews them to put herself in a positive mindset.

_____

_____

Model Step Eight: *Be patient with yourself*

Write down 5 affirmations to motivate and keep you focused.

_____

_____

Do not be too hard on yourself to complete each process, learn to take one step at a time, be patient when you feel frustrated to accomplish a goal. Be nice and gentle with yourself, as self-criticism will directly affect your idea achievement. You must learn to take time to celebrate your wins as you proceed.

Utilising The Power Of The Morning

Would you like to make better use of your morning?

Do you want to get more done quickly, easily and confidently in a day?

Discover the secret to organizing your day to achieving your ideas faster by using the power of the morning. There are 24 hours in a day, roughly half of that time you spend sleeping sometimes from 8pm-8am. By adjusting your sleep patterns; sleeping earlier and waking up earlier there's more to be fitted into your mornings. Waking up at 5:00am 3 hours earlier than usual there's so much you could do with those 3 hours for example a stay at home mother who wakes up at 5:00am could wash clothes, clean the house, cook breakfast and make packed lunches for her children. On the other hand, if she wakes up at 7:00am that only leaves 1 hour, limiting the number of activities she's able to achieve and as a result increasing the number of chores she'd have to do during the day.

For example, my 17-year-old daughter, she sleeps on average 10:00pm most nights and can sleep until 1:00pm. A few years ago, it was time for my children to go on holiday; their flight was an early flight. They went to sleep earlier in order to reduce tiredness for the journey ahead. Waking up at 3:00am we were able to drive to the airport, check-in and travel to an entirely different continent. I remember something my daughter said to me "Mummy normally by this time I would still be asleep, look at how much we've achieved just from adjusting our sleeping schedule". This is another example of the things you can accomplish just by pushing yourself to wake up just a little earlier.

If waking up earlier causes more fatigue, it's possible to fit in a time for napping. In the Italian culture, from about 12:30noon till 3.30pm evening businesses are closed, this is the time that traditionally was for siestas, sleeping during the afternoon. The streets became bare and entire towns turned to ghost towns.

Wake up early to Maximise your potential, plan your schedule for the day, layout your goals and to do list, Innovate, improve and excel. Learn to prioritise your activities; this will help you to avoid interruption. Forget your past mistakes, and conquer the things that have been holding you back, so you can set your priorities to double your productive and avoid procrastination to attain your focus on creating your ideas. Successful people with great ideas are experts in making quick decision to reach a strategic conclusion, focus on making things happen at all times and not waste time on issues that will distract your focus.

Tony Robbins described his intense morning routine, "breathing, expressing gratitude, praying and fuelling – having breakfast." He says that he does it because it changes the way he breathes and moves. Great achievers understand their mindset, capabilities and areas for improvement to attain their ideas. Learn to use this insight and knowledge to motivate yourself to think and stretch to reach for more. As you do this you'll enable yourself to grow to new height.

How to Make Vision Board for Your Idea

Make a vision board for your ideas where you put collection of pictures from old magazines, newspapers, etc of the images of things you desire to achieve to show your final Idea.

- Lay the pictures on the board

- Glue all the pictures on the board

- Add writing if you want

- Paint or write words with marker as desired.

- Ensure you put your own picture in the centre of the idea vision board where you look very happy with high expectancy.

- Put your vision board in a visible place where you will see it often.

This will help you focus and recharging you toward the achievement of your end idea and what you want manifest in your life. Visualise your idea as if it's already happening- in the present tense, what you focus on continuously expand.

How to Make Vision Board for Your Idea on computer

- Find pictures and images of your idea

- Open up a word document or power point, copy the images and save them in a folder

- Copy and paste the pictures from the folder

- Group them with a title

- Right Click each picture

- Click "format" tab

- Click "wrap" text

- Click "in front of"

- Arrange the pictures as desired

- Use as screen saver where you will see it more often

8 Tips to Achieve Your Ideas Faster

1. <u>Take full responsibility</u> and follow through with whatever it

takes to bring your vision into reality

2. <u>Develop a strong desire</u> to get things done in an exciting manner, not grudgingly

3. <u>Accept feedback</u> analysis by modifying your planned-action to improve your strategy.

4. <u>Don't quit</u>, keep pushing successful action steps daily

5. <u>Seek your creator's support and favour</u> for your vision plan to fulfill your purpose on earth.

6. <u>Appreciate and Celebrate</u> any little progress achieved on every step.

7. <u>Discipline</u> is the sustainer of your action, follow through your action plan, as an athlete would follow

set rules to keep the demanding training plan to win gold medal.

8. <u>Positive</u> action is the proof of vision; be proactive with possibility mindset.

Let the experience of great achievers inspire you to soar higher above fear, distraction, and self-doubt to follow through this tips.

Your decision on goal-setting today

What is your take when it comes to goal setting? Ask yourself these three questions.

- What have I decided on goal setting?

- If so, when should I make that decision?

- What exactly will I do?

Your Discipline Every Day

Based on the decision you have made on goal setting, what is the discipline you will practice daily to achieve your goal setting?

Transformation Action

Action is the key that will help you develop your ideas

- watch video studies on YouTube relating to your decision to help you grow

- discuss with those that can help you

- read short inspiration to help you start a habit to work with your idea

Look out for great opportunities to grow

Last words

"Give time, give space to spout your potential. Awaken the beautiful of your heart – the beauty of your spirit. There are infinite possibilities." – Amit Ray

Unlock your potential

My intention behind writing this little piece is to give you a solid framework through which to understand your power to develop your potential and ideas that could be worth millions. Have an idea to go with what works, trust your creative instincts, invest your time, money, focus on achieving your goals, and finding someone who can execute your ideas.

Many people commit suicide on a daily basis because they know so little about their capabilities and their potential; they have no idea who they really are, what they have within to develop an idea that can change lives of others and in turn give them financial freedom. You must be conscious about what you want to achieve; success is not going to happen overnight or by accident. As I explained in my book (Ikiriko 2013), success is not accidental but adequate cultivation of habits; properly worked out set goals, plans and diligent adherence to action plan. There is always a price to pay, which includes hard work and effort.

The little seed in you has the capacity to become a big tree that will yield many fruits if not crushed by fear, negligence or ignorance. If you indulge your fears, you risk burying your talent. Do not let your fear overtake you. Appreciate what you have, work every day with every opportunity that comes your way, and use your gifts and skills to generate an idea that can evolve into a business. Take control of what you have to turn your potential into a great idea that could generate your multiple stream of income.

Maximising your success is having the determination to discover and develop your own idea and work until you fulfill your purpose, even when you have fallen down. Have the knowledge of why ideas are important, listen to your inner voice to enable creativity and innovation from a simple thought to create an idea, and making a masterpiece of your life with the broken pieces; having the knowledge of where you are going and getting there, thereby fulfilling the purpose for your life.

You can decide to reach the impossible, develop resilience and strategy to overcome your limitations, model experts' ideas in your niche to be an extraordinary person. The development of your potential idea will bring you before great personalities and give you financial freedom.

Leverage opportunities; uncover practical ways to break through boundaries of self-limiting beliefs, envision your end result to create the right path to achieve ideas faster.

Persistence and consistence is the mark of champions who have changed the world. Let the experience of great achievers inspire you to soar higher above fear, distraction, and self-doubt to set your goals and action plan to accomplish your ideas. You can make the most of your potential as you desire and dare to stand in spite of all odds to make it. Great achievers have to contend with challenges in the pursuit of their ideas. However, through persistence, they were able to come up with wonderful ideas that have changed the world. Anyone who wants to be successful must accept this as part of the deal. Persevering is not often convenient – you will be squeezed, you will be roughened up, you will be disappointed, looked down upon, and some people may think you are insane. As described by Jessie Hartland in "her inspirational version of the 'insanely great' of Steve Job as a misfit who refused to follow the rules or play well with others, who was as rebellious as he was smart". But that is a certain path for anyone in the quest of unique ideas to succeed. In life nothing of value is free. If so, success is all about added value, subsequently it must carry definite price.

This book is about helping you to accept real responsibility, for the success of those dream ideas that you have. It was Thaila that said, "I think nothing is impossible when you want to fulfil a dream. A lot of people will tell you that you can't do it, that you don't have what it takes, but if it is in your heart and you feel it, there is nothing that will stop you. It is like the sun – you can't block it: it will shine regardless, if that is what you want". If this little book succeeds in inspiring you to discover those potentials to develop your unique ideas, then my purpose for writing it would have been achieved.

You are gifted with creative ability; you are an asset created with great **Idea** that can launch you into the world of exploit to create multiple streams of income to gain financial freedom

You can make it when you try!

Transformation Action

Action is the key that will help you develop your ideas

- watch video studies on YouTube relating to your decision to help you grow

- discuss with those that can help you

- read short inspiration to help you start a habit to work with your idea

Look out for great opportunities to grow

References

'Bill Gates' (2016). <u>Wikipedia</u>. Available at: <u>https://en.wikipedia.org/wiki/Bill Gates</u> (Accessed: 8 September 2016).

Cherryman, B. (2015). Retired teacher who overcome adversity to inspire children to achieve their dream for more than 40 years remembered. <u>Watford Observer</u>, 2 October. Available at: <u>http://www.watfordobserver.co.uk/news/13799691.Retired teacher who overcame adversity to inspire children to achieve their dreams for more than 40 years remembered/Watford</u>Observer [online newspaper] (Accessed 5 October 2016).

Dicks. J, W, Hansen. M, V., & Nanton. N. (2015). <u>Boom!</u> USA: Celebrity Press. Available at: <u>https://www.amazon.co.uk/Boom-Nick-Nanton-Esq/dp/0990706478</u> (Accessed: 29 September 2016)

Hartland, J. (2015). Steve Jobs: Insanely Great. Available at: <u>https://www.kirkusreviews.com/book-reviews/jessie-hartland/steve-jobs-insanely-great/</u> (Accessed: 30 October 2017).

Hill, N. (1960). Think and Grow Rich. Fawcett Books, New York. Available at:

https://en.wikipedia.org/wiki/Think_and Grow Rich (Accessed: 16 May 2016).

Ikiriko, O. P. (2015) Becoming Self-Confident. Available: https://www.amazon.com/Becoming-Self-Confident-thoughts-define-success/dp/1514342707/

Ikiriko, O. P. (2013). The Successful Student. London: Panoma Press

Lewthwaite, J., & Miscandlon, S. (2012) Getting Things Done in Business. {Online}. Available: https://www.amazon.co.uk/dp/B008P4W 9CA. (Accessed: 8 September 2012)

Munroe. M, & Kinchlow, B. (1992). In pursuit of purpose. USA: Destiny Image.

'Pablo Picasso' (2016). Wikipedia. Available at: https://en.wikipedia.org/wiki/Pablo_Picasso (Accessed: 8 September 2016).

'Steve Jobs' (2016). Wikipedia. Available at: https://en.wikipedia.org/wiki/Steve_Jobs (Accessed: 8 September 8, 2016).

'The Popsicle Was Invented By An 11 Year Old' (2016). Today I found Out: Feed Your Brain. Available at:http://www.todayifoundout.com/index.php/2011/08/the-popsicle-was-invented-by-an-11-year-old/ (Accessed: 5 September 2016).

'Top 10 Under 20: 10 Teenagers Who Changed the World in 2013' (2013). The Richest. Available at: http://www.therichest.com/rich-list/most-influential/top-10-under-20-10-teenagers-who-changed-the-world-in-2013/ (Accessed: 2 September 2016).

'8 amazing kids who have changed the world' (2015).HISTORY.com. Available at:http://www.history.com/topics/inventions/alexander-graham-bell (Accessed: 19 May 2016).

'10 Amazing Inventions by Teens' (2014). Oddee. Available at:

http://www.oddee.com/item_99064.aspx (Accessed: 16 May 2016).

'8 kid entrepreneurs to watch' (2011). CNN Money International. Available at: http://money.cnn.com/galleries/2011/sm allbusiness/1105/gallery.kid entrepreneu rs/8.html (Accessed: 8 September 2016).

'How Mark Zuckerberg Started: The Life of Facebook's Founder' (2014) Funders and Founders. Available at: http://fundersandfounders.com/how-mark-zuckerberg-started/ (Accessed: 16 May 2016).

BOOKS BY PATRICIA ORLUNWO IKIRIKO

You Can Be Richer Than Your Parents

The Successful
Student

The Successful
Student

Workbook

Becoming
Self-
Confident

Young and
Influential

ABOUT THE AUTHOR

 Patricia is The CEO and Founder of Young and Influential, Inc. dedicated to developing leadership and wealth building skills in young people. She is a trained counsellor, author, entrepreneur, life coach and inspirational speaker. For over 18 year, she continue to expand her horizons, despite the challenging obstacles with today's young people and the economy

A prolific writer, Amazon Bestseller, She has a Master of Philosophy in Psychology from University of Bedfordshire, United Kingdom, a Graduate Diploma in

Psychology from the University Of East London, a Master's degree in Education Guidance and Counselling from the University of Port Harcourt, Rivers State, Nigeria, a B.Ed. in Guidance, Counselling and Psychology from University Of Ibadan, Nigeria and a National Certificate in Education from the University Of Ibadan Nigeria.

Her passion and goal is to help young people develop their potential to implementing ideas that aren't taught in school into producing products and marketing them, to create their own business and wealth channel.

She is married to Hon (Evang) Hope Odhuluma Ikiriko and blessed with two children, four foster children, and four grandchildren.